Holocaust o

(A Theory about the Cri

Members of Agent Parties in Iraq)

Prof. Dr. Maan Khalil Al-Omar

Reviewer: Jihan Asim Al-Taie

Translator: Kais As-Sultany

Table of Contents

Dedication

To the patriotic offerings that sacrificed their lives in
defence of the soil of Iraq and its people against its rulers,
the agents of the coloniser

About the Author

Professor Maan Khalil Al Omar is one of the most prominent Middle Eastern sociologists known for his research and theories about the stratification of the Middle Eastern and Arabic societies and their interaction with other societies. He is a theorist of Arab sociology and the founder of the theory "Towards an Arab Sociology".

He is a highly qualified researcher and theorist. He received his Bachelor of Arts degree in Sociology from Baghdad University in 1965, then he obtained a Master's degree in Sociology from Eastern Michigan University, USA, in 1968, and culminated his academic studies in 1976 by obtaining a PhD degree in sociology from Wayne State University, Michigan, USA.

His rich career journey as an assistant professor began in the College of Arts, Department of Sociology, University of Baghdad, where he progressed until he reached the rank of Professor in 1988. Besides his work in Baghdad University, he taught sociology at Muhammad bin Abdullah in Morocco, Yarmouk University - Jordan, Emirates University - United Arab Emirates, and Naif University - Saudi Arabia. Currently, he is an advisor to many governments as well as to non-government organisations in the Middle East, focusing on the development of different social aspects in these societies.

He has written a staggering 70 books and published more than 50 studies on various social topics covering the sociology of crime, juvenile crimes, family, education, youth, childhood, women, poverty, and the sociology of revolution. His writings varied between theories, methods, applications, and fields of sociology, focusing on the critical and evaluative aspects of contemporary social events. His latest publication – the dialectic of the individual and society in sociology – is an outstanding read in which he clarifies a new horizon in the development of sociology science with the development of human societies.

Introduction

Since the onset of the American occupation of Iraq in 2003, Iraqi society has experienced various drastic changes which would appear as normal reactions to the occupation as it happened throughout history with other societies. Therefore, at least one of the currently available social theories dealing with such conditions would be applicable to the Iraqi situation and to its future developments. Unfortunately, that was not the case here. Iraqi conditions and the imposed setup seemed to be unique where no social theory was found applicable. Accordingly, it became a necessity to formulate a new theory that can model and accommodate the current and future social changes of Iraq. This theory may be generalised to avoid its conditions' manifestation to other nations subject to similar unjust occupation or when a social disorder is intentionally created and imposed by influential powers within these nations. This is true as recent evidence showed that the Iraqi model was copied and manifested in certain Middle Eastern and North African countries where all or most of its painful and destructive consequences were implemented, leaving the poor people of these countries in deep suffering while the criminals continued in harvesting the benefits of their crimes unlawfully.

Within the context of this book, a new social theory that was developed for the Iraqi conditions is presented. This theory stems from a comprehensive analysis and insight vision of the Iraqi society after the 2003 American occupation. Upon such occupation, the Iraqi governing system was transformed from a totalitarian regime to a scattered sectarian and tribal regime. In this transformation, a stable social order was changed to cancerous chaos utilising all occupation associated events that occurred and played effective roles in replacing security and safety by violence and terrorism, reorienting the national identity of the Iraqi society to unprecedented sectarian and tribal identification, and altering the highly controlled one-ruling party setup to multiple parties controlled by and loyal to Iran but disguised in religion and tribe while receiving full blessing and support of the American unreasonably. Meanwhile, the integrity has disappeared and swapped by corruption which sabotaged the basic foundations of Iraqi society constructive patterns and empowering factional parties who were double agents of Iran and America and who have adopted sectarianism to tear of the Iraqi society. These parties acted as the dirty hand of the double jointly synchronised and coordinated occupation by the American and the Iranian. Such a fact might not have been very clear to the Iraqi people and to the rest of the world earlier, but it became much clearer later as it was realised beyond any

2

doubt that, after toppling the Iraqi regime and eliminating every resistance to the unjust occupation, the American handed over Iraq to Iran as a gift to milk out its wealth and natural resources unlawfully, destroying the Iraqi society, humiliating Iraqi people and denying them living in peace and rebuilding their country. Such a handover was either a stupid uncalculated action by the American Administration or has been done on purpose to allow the parties loyal to Iran to carry out the Persians and Americans revenge from the Iraqi people who opposed them and repelled their hatred against Iraq.

On top of being official thieves, the leaders and members of the Iranian loyal parties were and continue to be criminals, killers, and agents to foreigners against what supposed to be their country. All Iraqi governments that have been formed since the American occupation and up to the present have got the American agreement and blessing, and without exception, all of them were governments of kleptocrats (a bunch of traitors, thieves, and murderers). They are strangers to the Iraqi people, and most of them are of Iranian origin with forged Iraqi nationality. They were beggars before the occupation living on the social security aids of Europe, the UK and the USA and suddenly became rich and wealthy as they stole the wealth of Iraq and its people under the eyes and with full knowledge of the American officials. They behave like emperors steeling and donating the wealth of

Iraqi people to foreigners as if they have inherited such wealth. They got the legitimacy from the religious clerks to do whatever they like with stolen wealth, whether to spend it on their families, entertainment, gambling or bribery to buy loyalty and support for their personal status and their parties instead of financing the promised undelivered programs of reforming Iraq. The country was destroyed by the American occupation and before that by the international blockade imposed on Iraq since Kuwait problem in 1991. In effect, the after-occupation rulers of Iraq were not Iraqi nationals but a mongrel of spiteful and vengeful foreigners. They were not faithful to the independence of Iraq or its financial and natural wealth and have skillfully mastered the theft and betrayed Iraq, considering the treason to Iraq and its people as an honour for them to be proud of openly. Moreover, they capitalised on the sectarian nature of Iraqi society to make sectarianism and tribalism a necessary condition for their rule converting Iraq to a major victim that it has never witnessed in its ancient and modern history. They formed armed militias to protect them rather than acting to protect Iraq. Their criminality was a compound of several types (moral, religious, institutional, and political). That was the norm for them and did not surprise anyone because they have no honourable political past and no sincere national affiliation. They fought against Iraq and Iraqis and aligned with the foreign countries against Iraq.

4

Hence they replaced non-standardisation for a period of seventeen-odd years. They emptied its coffers and made its land an arena for international conflicts. They used their arms against all those who did not agree with them, and in spite of witnessing their rejection by Iraqi people through the repeated uprisings of millions, they continue to acknowledge and have pride in their treason, corruption and crimes without shame. Although they behave as emperors in Iraq, they are cheap mules and tails of Iran and America. We infer from the foregoing that they represent a government that directly exports treachery to all members of society without exception with intentional and unintended neglect by its ministries, preferring the interests of its parties and militias which tamper the stability of the homeland and not obeying the laws—sabotaging the industries of Iraq, wasting its money, drying up its rivers, and destroying its agriculture for the benefit and service of the Iranian government. Not because they are agents, but because they have no loyalty to Iraq and are adept at fraud, deceit and cunning in appropriating other people's money and raping state property, which they consider as war spoils while pretending to be committed to religion and tribal affiliation, but they do not value the people of religion and tribe.

It seemed that the systematic structural and organisational destruction of the Iraqi society was not enough to fulfil their revenge desire, so they went further in their humiliating style. They insulted the doctrines that they impersonated while became very fanatic about their tribes and isolated the Iraqi society from its sovereignty, so they were the best agents of the spiteful foreigners. They installed the rabble in the place of competencies in professional and institutional activities, widened the economic gap between them and the citizens, raised the level of the high cost of living and held on to male power against women. To weaken Iraq as a country, they dismantled the most professional Iraqi army and turned it into a mercenary army unqualified to defend the homeland, and brought thousands of Iranians and Kurds from Syria, Turkey, and Iran to settle in Iraq to support their various crimes of murder, plunder, and displacement, with total negligence to Iraqi scholars and thinkers to evacuate Iraq from its talented people. They forced the Iraqis to live below the poverty line, a life that represents a pre-industrial stage, lacking electricity, drinking water, hygiene, and safety, while they kept filling their pockets and diverting their thefts abroad for fear of their end in the hands of the Iraqis. They did not fear the religion or the will of the Iraqis to change and reform the situation because they are obsessed with stealing public money though it is religiously forbidden.

After this digression, I must refer to the victims of government crime that are committed by sectarian parties which do not concern Iraqi individuals only, but the entire

Iraqi society becomes a victim of their criminality. All of those who do not support or follow but oppose the armed militia become the natural target to be killed and displaced. Such crimes became the norm in Iraqi streets. Since the criminal is known to be a thief and a murderer, he faces resistance from the victim, so he carries arms to defend himself and kill the victim. This was one of the reasons given by the ruling parties for forming armed militias for them from the patriots of the Persian and Americans to kill and displace their opponents. However, the other hidden reason is that these militias are the Iranian hand in Iraq, as stated by the leaders of these militias expressing their readiness to execute any criminal act outside Iran to assure the control of Iran on Iraq and other counties in the Middle East. This is a clear threatening to other sovereign countries from Iraq homeland and disturbing the peace in the area. The third reason is to use these militias as balancing paper in the negotiation with the Americans while Iraq and its people pay the bill for the recklessness and the aggressive adventures of Iran because of these militias.

It took revenge on the Iraqis on behalf of the greatest enemy of Iraq, who had fought for eight years in the first gulf between 1980 and 1988. Having said that, such an act of revenge is meaningless and unjustified unless it has other hidden hostilities. This is true because the previous regime which oppressed the currently ruling parties was overthrown, its party was uprooted, and the Iraqi army that fought against their beloved Iran was dissolved, while the Iranian revenge against the Iraqi society continued via their armed militia by plundering Iraq wealth and corrupting its institutions, so they played hostile and avenger role even after the demise of the regime which persecuted and displaced them. Therefore, the criminality of the ruling parties is complex and considered to be a collective crime that has no justification other than killing Iraqis, displacing them, and robbing them of their wealth. They continued in this manner for seventeen more years. They were not satisfied with assassinating the victims and stealing their money, but due to their ignorance, lack of patriotism and their greed for public money, they worked to assassinate Iraq scholars, thinkers and leaders who highlighted the name of Iraq and who are its scientific and historical ammunition. They did not think about their future because this is the first time in the history of Iraq that the Shias and the Kurds are governing it. They revealed their lack of patriotism, fanatic hatred, impartiality and lack of integrity and honesty towards Iraq coupled with lack of experience in all elements of government and international relations. Instead of protecting the Iraqis and providing them with services, the Iraqis have misled, tormented, and robbed of their will and money. They, therefore, gave a sincere impression of the treason their parties have exercised due to the lack of patriotism.

They proved beyond doubt that they are not qualified to lead the enlightened Iraqi people who are aware of Iraq history. Instead of reforming and rebuilding Iraq, these traitors created a mess that had never been witnessed by Iraqis. They are, therefore, criminals par excellence against society and not against the specific individual, against civilians and not against politicians, against the reputation and integrity of Iraqis and their dignity and against the values of the Islamic religion. They are cowards because they sought refuge with a foreigner throughout their rule, and they were armed with armed gangs to protect them instead of seeking refuge in the army or its security institutions. Because they do not have a collective base in Iraq, they abused the Iraqis openly and admitted that they are corrupt and murderers without any worry of prosecution by the government as they are the government. This is a very strange setup that America has created in Iraq as such a setup and ugliness cannot be found anywhere else. However, the Iraqis have rejected their rule, revolted against them, and waiting for the day when they are held accountable and judged unmercifully for all the crimes they have committed against the Iraqi people. Therefore, they fabricated sectarian strife and received assistance from the Iranian government to help them cover up their criminality because they are known to be patriotic to Iran and stigmatised with treason and criminality against the Iraqis. They are heavy-weight criminals who steal billions of dollars, smuggling Iraqi oil and stealing the state revenues from its borders' outlets. They persisted in stealing everything, and their lowliness has reached theft of salaries of employees, retirees, and the income support of those who are on social security aids. They represent an organised criminal gang composed of non-disciplined elements which do not abide by the applicable laws of Iraqi society whose interests are based on fraud. They do not hesitate to kill their victims to achieve what they are aiming for and what they are coveting from the Iranian government, and this is what made them use armed militias to satisfy their greed and treachery and avenge the Iranian government. The most prominent victims of the Iraqi government's crime are the following:

Banks and financial institutions, including the central bank.

1.   Human legacy (rare treasures).

2.   Human smuggling.

3.   Child trafficking.

4.   Slave trade.

5.   sabotage of property.

I would not end this introduction without referring to the ethics of thieves in the Islamic civilisation in the late second and early third century AH (during the Abbasid era), particularly the gangs of rappels and savages, who had conventions among them that forbid theft of the poor people, women, and neighbours, while allowing gangs robbing the

10

markets and the homes of the rich people only. As for the current rulers of Iraq, they do not even have the morals of those thieves centuries ago. They have no differentiation between the poor and rich people. They steal the money from the poor, women, and neighbours but rather displace them from their areas, which means that they are at the most disgraceful and inferior level of the thieves as compared to those of the second century AH.

At the end of my introduction, I would like to express my sincere thanks and gratitude to my wife, Mrs Jihan Asim Al-Taie, for reviewing this book and putting forth serious notes on it. Her intellectual and performance efforts are highly appreciated and praised. My thanks and appreciation also go to Dr Kais As-Sultany for his efforts in translating this book from Arabic to English language and for the help he has extended for the publishing of the book. Finally, I ask Al-Mighty God, who has given all the right and its existence, to guide our steps and to culminate in our endeavour with success and to guide us to knowledge, which is our first and last goal in all that we pursue and strive for.

Theoretical Concepts

Each social theory has its procedural and theoretical concepts extracted from the nature of the studied community, and since this theory deals with Iraqi society after the American occupation and Iranian sponsorship since 2003, new social phenomena have emerged that were not prevalent or known among Iraqis, which are the following: -

1. Emperors: this is a satirical label to describe the controllers and monopolies who became experts in defying the law. They are arrogant, tyrants and have excessive pride because they have been given a status way above their actual capability and competency.

2. State crimes: are the crimes that the state committed against its own citizens and carrying out prohibited acts such as violating human rights, mass killing and arbitrariness in judging its subjects and citizens, and practising fanaticism and sectarian, religious, and ethnic discrimination among citizens. In 2003, Kazula and his colleagues proposed several main keys to defining state crimes, namely:

   a. When material, moral, or bodily harm or damage is caused by any of the governmental organisations towards individuals, groups, or their representatives.

b. When harm, damage, or abuse to the people is caused directly by an authorised and responsible personal holding one of the government positions.

c. When neglect takes place (intentional or unintentional) by the state institutions or their representatives.

d. When personal interests, especially the interests of the ruling elite who is controlling the state, are given preference over the interests of the public.

3. Rides (Tails): who are voluntary making themselves available for others to ride them like the animals that are used as a means of transportation to reach certain goals and targets.

4. The national identity: a set of values and morals that are manifested in actions concerning the stability of the homeland, its defence, compliance with its regulations, and respect of its laws. Its components include language, culture, loyalty to the homeland, facing challenges, coexistence, and attachment to the place.

5. Identity impersonation: assumption of a false identity by a person from a public authority to claim what he has not got. For others, it is like claiming victimhood and impersonating its characteristics

while they are the oppressor rather than the oppressed.

6. Strength gaining from a foreigner: throwing themselves in the cuddle of the foreigner to gain power. Political Islam does not mind bullying others using and inviting the foreigner to interfere in the affairs of the homeland if it enables him to gain power. The Shiite and Kurdish parties fought with the foreign armies (Iranian, American, and British) against the Iraqi National Army and the national government in order to overthrow them to gain power rather than defending Iraq.

7. Agents to the foreigners: those who are involved in high treason or espionage, in which the agent mastered treachery, ingratitude and selling himself to the enemies of the country. He cooperates with the enemies and provides them with dangerous information that reveals strategic state secrets and threatening security. He also carries out sabotage acts and helps the enemies' armies in fighting and destroying his country's army. As treason in Iraq has become the norm, and it is loudly practised, all agents have occupied top sovereign positions, and they enjoy the security services provided to them. They rally with their masters and the tails inside Iraq. To confirm their treason, they labelled the streets,

shops, and roads in names of their Iranian masters without feeling shame.

8. Customary non-standardisation: where the rulers of Iraq after 2003 have transformed the natural social standards into non-normality through their formal practices with customary. For example, they consider theft as an art, forgery as a cleverness. They used killing as normal customary, and bribery as facilitation. They brag about their treason as if it is an honour, and they have the right to feel proud about it. In their customary, the plundering is a golden opportunity that has been granted to them as far as they are in power where all the country wealth became in their hand. On the other hand, the treachery that they are continuously practising is their best craft. They stick to the racism and count it as part of the inter-relation between them, and on the same page, they converted the clans to an official authority.

Iraqi Agents Ranted Publicity for Iran and America

The Iraqi case is strange by all measures and has not happened or practised anywhere in the world. The concept of treason here is used differently and has risen to the highest level, and goes beyond the well-known concept. Such a level represents the greatest treason - by negative preference – in its intense hostility to the homeland and the people. It is coupled with the full cooperation with the foreigner to destroy every aspect of Iraqis life. The killing of citizens does not stop at a certain limit. No, it is extended to all associates around him, including family, relatives, and friends. It is the selling and leasing of the homeland, the people, and the conscience. In general, it is the abandonment of all social values of patriotism, morals and legitimacy, like a defected soldier who flees from his army during a battle, joining the enemy and handing over all critical military information about his country's army to the enemy. Is there any treason greater than this? Thus, what happened and continue to happen in Iraq is great treason. When someone voluntarily joins the enemy, fights against his country's army, and participates in effective military operations against it without being concerned that perhaps his brother, son, or relative is standing on the other side defending his homeland, this is the greatest treason. Also, when someone is holding a high position in his country as a minister, member of parliament or a military commander while his religious and political belief is linked to a hostile party, this is the greatest treason. And when he is in such a highly influential position and declares that in the event of a war between his country and a neighbouring country, he will stand with the neighbouring country and fight against his people, this is the greatest treason. The best example of such treason is when the former minister and head of the Badr bloc in the Iraqi parliament (Hadi Al-Amiri) and before him the Iraqi Hezbollah leader Wathiq Al-Battat, stated that they would stand with Iran if a war erupted with Iran because they received orders from Khamenei; so that is the matter. It becomes clear that it is not related to a sectarian doctrine like imitation or performing the duties as some think. No, it is a political doctrine that has major repercussions for Iraq. It is obvious that anyone becomes an agent to a foreign country when he is trying his best to keep it secret because such a crime will be judged by capital punishment or life imprisonment if his dirty conduct is discovered by the security authorities of his country. Moreover, the agent is supposed to practice the best cases of concealment and disguise, and often hostile intelligence forces support him in this matter through training courses, observing his movements, and alerting him to any mistake he makes, no matter how slight. However, Iraq is the only country in the world in which agents practice their betrayal openly in daylight and declare their treason to the media without the slightest embarrassment.

Iraq is the only country in the world where treason is awarded rather than punished. The traitors in Iraq occupy sovereign positions as ministers, heads of blocs in the House of Representatives and members of Parliament, and Iraq is the only country in the world that hands over the presidency of its security services to agents of other countries such as Faleh Al-Fayyad who is Iranian veteran occupying the head of the National Security Agency position. Iraq is also the only country in the world where agents meet their security and political leaders from hostile countries on its soil. Iranian General Soleimani, before his killing, was meeting with Iraqi agents inside Iraq rather than in Iran and in public without any warning from the President of the Republic of Iraq, its government, or its parliament as they do not dare to warn about this issue that affects the sovereignty of Iraq. We say stop this anomalous phenomenon because they are too weak to stand before the Iranian general. Similarly, the President of Iraq and the President of the Iraqi Parliament visited the Iranian ambassador in Iraq to grant them his blessing and selecting them to these positions as if he is the actual governor of Iraq. Also, Iraq is the only country in the world where agents raise pictures and banners of the leaders of the countries that recruited them and name the streets and roads

18

after their names, such as Khomeini Street in Basra even though this province gave thousands of martyrs in the Iran-Iraq war that was extended by the buried Khomeini (the disgraceful) for more than eight years. An anomaly that the human mind cannot imagine. And the strange thing is that the Basra Provincial Council, which is controlled by traitors, decided to set up a shrine in the place where Khomeini use to urinate and performed ablution!!!

This is the case of Iraq for those who do not know it or are inclined to believe the views of the politicised Iraqi and foreign media. Iraq is subject to the command of the Iranian Guardianship of the Jurist as it is the main player, followed by the Americans. As for the rest of the neighbouring countries and the Gulf states, there is exaggeration regarding their interference in Iraqi affairs, the purpose of which is to strike a balance with the Iranian interference. The truth is that the Gulf states have absolutely no influence on Iraqi affairs. Who is concerned about the formation of the Iraqi government and complete the quorum of the ministerial cabinets? The Iranian ambassador is and not the Saudi ambassador or any Gulf or Turkish party.

Iraq is the only country that includes military forces that are not under the control of the prime minister and commander-in-chief of the armed forces but rather under the authority of a neighbouring country. So, the so-called Popular Mobilization Forces is a grouping of militias linked to Iran, and the deputy head of the Popular Mobilization Authority, Abu Mahdi Al-Muhandis, on 10th December 2018 demanded the government and the Iraqi parliament to allocate "a distinguishable budget for the members of the Islamic Resistance to implement Imam Khomeini project, in order to build camps and equip the crowd with appropriate weapons and basic equipment|". Therefore, your sons in the Popular Mobilization Authority, which belongs to Ayatollah Khamenei, are Khamenei's soldiers, not the soldiers of the Prime Minister and Commander-in-Chief of the Armed Forces, Adel Abdul Mahdi, who did not dare to utter a single word about this insult, as he swallowed it on an empty stomach without a dose of water. In fact, they are used to swallowing insults, and this is the case with the agents. Do you know the reality of Iraq today and who rules it? Do you know the truth about the so-called popular crowd and whose loyalty is? Do you know the truth of Hadi Al-Ameri, who is called by the Iraqi media (Sheikh of the Mujahideen), is in fact (the sheikh of the agents)? Do you know that the disgraced Sunnis who allied with Hadi Al-Ameri are guinea pigs (laboratory specimens) in the presence of the Guardian of the Jurist? Do you know that the Mufti of Iraq (Mahdi Al-Sumaida'i), Khaled Al-Mulla, Abdul-Latif Al-Hamim, and Abdul-Ghafour Al-Samarrai are pawns on the Guardian of the Jurist chessboard? They do not deserve a slap by slipper for fear that the slipper will be contaminated by touching their dirty faces. As for some of the Shiite religious authorities, they are exposed as agents and do not need a mask to disguise their loyalty to Iran. We hope that the trick will not be deceiving to the wise people in that the Shiite reference Ali Al-Sistani does not believe in the Guardianship of the Jurist, as the words are denied by actions. If the Guardian of the jurist in Iran practices religious and political affairs openly, then he also practices religious and political affairs in Iraq, once in public and once under the table, starting from writing the constitution and voting on it and urging participation in previous electoral sessions and recommending the corrupt under the pretext of supporting the sect, and hastening the formation of the government, the one who made the fifteen judges recount the votes in the recent rigged elections to quickly finish their work in response to the authority's request, and to nominate Adel Abdul Mahdi as prime minister, given that he has been experimented several times. All this means that the Guardianship of the Jurist in Iraq and Iran has no dispute between them in terms of substance. Every disgrace can be washed except the disgrace of betrayal, for it is an eternal disgrace. It is like chronic diseases accompanying the agents to their humiliated graves and then inherited by their descendants as a heavy legacy covered with shame and disgrace, as it was inherited by the descendants of Ibn Al-Alqami, Al-Tusi, Abu Rghal and other traitors of the nation.

Every betrayal can be forgiven except the betrayal of the homeland, as its eternal curse will be like a black cloud that shadows the graves of traitors for generations to come! The smell of every carrion will disappear with the passage of days, except for the carrion of betrayal. The more time passes, the more its nasty smell spreads and the more harmful it becomes, so says the history of nations, not just ours. And history is the laboratory of living peoples. The only good for the occupation is that it revealed to us the truth about the agents who came on the back of its tanks carrying all the seeds of evil, discord and sectarianism to plant them in the sacred soil of Iraq and fertilise them by the best Iranian fertilisers to produce bundles of poisonous thorns. The fact that these agents will pay a high price for their alliance with the Great and Lesser Satan has been revealed. The hour of reckoning will be closer to them than their eyelids, and their reckoning is not from their victims only, but from the entire Iraqi people, after the people wake up from the opium of religious references that destroyed Iraq. The agents, before taking power, claimed from their American masters that their hostility was with the previous national government system only! Then it became clear that the hostility is with the homeland and the people, not just with the regime! The Iraqi parliament is supposed to abolish the article of high treason from the Iraqi Penal Code, Article / 111, if it does not apply to its members, especially since there are heads of parties and representatives in Parliament to whom this article applies. At the very least, these traitors can be exempted from the application of this article to their treason as it happened to corrupt officials who stole billions of dollars from Iraq and fled abroad. There is no good in a country where theft became an art, and the forgery is an intelligence, plunder is an opportunity, treachery is a craft, murder is a customary, bribery is facilitation, tribalism is authority, sectarianism is a necessity, racism is love, and betrayal is an honour. And there is no good in a country where agents, criminals, and mobs from the Rafha camp are honoured with three salaries, even the infant among them, on the grounds that they were mujahideen, although the reward for jihad is with God, as it is assumed, and not with the government. There is no good in a country where the agent brags about his treason and declares himself an agent? I do not think anyone ruled Iraq since the time of Prophet Lut until now worse than the current leaders (traitors) of Iraq.

Crime Categories of the Traitor Parties

The crimes of the traitor parties that ruled Iraq for seventeen years since 2003 can be classified into the following categories:

A. Crimes Against People

1. Assassination of Iraqi scholars, intellectuals, pilots, and military leaders who fought Iran before 2003.

2. Killing of national activists who came out expressing corruption of the rulers, stealing public money and impersonation of the Jaafari sect.

3. Assassination of national media professionals.

4. Assassination of Baathist party members and leaders of the Sunni community.

B. Crimes Against Iraqi Property and Wealth

1. Theft of central bank funds (gold and foreign currencies)

2. Smuggling of classified documents and humanity historical monuments from the museums and security services of Iraq.

3. Theft of Iraqi banks' funds (Al-Rafidain banks).

4. Theft of state real estate property.

5. Theft of state lands and their distribution among the affiliates of the client parties.

6. Theft of Iraqi army weapons.

7. Stealing oil, smuggling it abroad and receiving its price.

8. Theft of state resources of border crossings and their sharing among armed militias affiliated with traitors' parties.

9. Blowing up mosques and imams' shrines.

10. Diversion of river courses from Iraqi lands to Iranian lands.

11. Concluding illusory contracts and projects and seizing their funds.

12. Practice of money laundering.

13. Public auction of hard currency and its smuggling abroad.

C. Crimes Against the Iraqi Society

1. Displacement of Sunni tribes and families from their areas of residence.

2. Igniting sectarian strife between Sunnis and Shiites.

3. Killing worshipers in Sunni mosques by storming them during prayer.

4. Exercising violence and terror against civilians.

5. Segregating the Sunni areas from the Shiites by concrete walls.

6. Spreading drugs of Iranian source among youth.

7. Spreading illiteracy that Iraq had eliminated before their rule.

8. Making the Iraqis live below the poverty line.

9.   Settling Iranians in Iraq and granting them Iraqi nationality.

10.   Settling the Kurds of Iran, Turkey, and Syria in the Kurdish regions.

11.   Selling of arrested boys with the intention of practicing sexual deviation.

12.   Encouraging prostitution by legitimising the temporary enjoyment marriage.

13.   Substituting non-standardisation in place of the value standardised normality in social control.

14.   Spreading institutional corruption and disrupting the implementation of regulations in it.

15.   Theft of retirees' salaries

16.   The demolition of the middle-class population pyramid by displacing it outside Iraq and making it consist of the broad base of the poor - the lowest class, and at the top a parasitic class of members of the agents and tails parties and their militia leaders.

17.   Distorting the reputation of the Shiite community in Iraq and making it focus only on sectarian practices that the Jaafari doctrine does not support (such as Slapping, funeral processions, striking the head with swords, plunge into muds, etc.)

18.   Party militia replacing the army and police in security.

19. Granting documents of Iraqi nationality to Iranian agents.

20. Supporting Iranian trade at the expense of the Iraqi economy to save Iran's collapsing economy under sanction.

21. Feeding the army, police and security forces with the phantom aliens and receiving their salaries.

22. Establishing of the deep state in each of the Iraqi ministries.

23. Eliminating safety and security in the daily life of Iraqis.

24. Cutting off electricity for long periods of time every day.

25. Committing espionage on phone calls and social media.

26. Dumping the Iraqi markets with bad and corrupt Iranian goods at the expense of Iraqi goods and Iraqi agriculture and industry.

The main objective behind showing the crimes of the Iraqi rulers is to highlight that these crimes have not been committed by smart criminals, professional politicians, or religious people who believe in religion and the sect. Rather, they have been carried out by stupid individuals and groups that do not know how to use their minds, and they are not more than rides and tails, driven by their riders and their leaders, the Iranians and the Americans who plan and program these types of crimes in order to revenge from the Iraqis and Iraq. If they were smart enough, they would think about what would happen to them after the theft and murder? Why should they have armed militias funded by the Iranian and American governments? Besides what has been mentioned earlier that these militias provide some sort of security to the traitors, their main objective, in fact, is to revenge from Iraq as they are the dirty hand of Iran and America. This is a gang dedicated to acting against Iraqi society, its property, and its history. There were no bloody or confrontational disputes between the parties because their actions and conduct were dictated from the outside by Iran and America. They do not have a political or national program because they are neither politicians nor Iraqi patriots. Rather, they are enemies of Iraq and the executors of the hatred of the Iranian and American governments. Before the toppling of the Baathist regime in 2003, they were trying to justify their crimes as an act of revenge from Baathists, but after 2003 and when the Iraqi army and its security systems were dismantled, these crimes cannot be considered other than revenge from the Iraqis by the Iranian rides and the tails represented by the militias which are sponsored and instructed by Iran and America. These are the most important rulers of the agent parties of Iran and America in Iraq, but they will face their insulting and humiliating end to them, their followers, and their likes in

Iraq at the hands of the conscious citizens of their own countrymen before others. That is true because Iran and America could not inflict harm on Iraqis without using these traitors whose crimes even exceeded the crimes of Iran and America together collectively against Iraq. In their crimes, the agents were and are worse than anyone can imagine. They know nothing but treason, crime, theft, and what have been provided and proved in the context of this book. The traitors' crimes and their parties can be classified as follows:

1. White collar's crimes: those who have assumed high and sovereign positions in ministries and government agencies are only proficient in fraud, forgery, deception, abuse of positions, theft, smuggling, embezzlement, bribery, extortion, and the sale and purchase of government's positions.

2. Crimes of white and black turbans (religion clerics): these are committed by those impersonating clerics in the Shiite and Sunni communities, who are good at issuing false fatwas to legitimise forbidden things and explaining trivial religious issues which do not do anything to Iraq problems. On the contrary, without the fatwa of their top reference, the popular crowd and hence the militias formulation would not have been justified.

3. Militia crimes: these are committed by the militias who know nothing but murder, assassination, rape,

and terrorism, and they are unemployed, demobilised from the former army, poor and illiterate.

All of them do not know the reconstruction, construction, development, building of the homeland and its recovery from the devastation that befell Iraq. Finally, it can be stated that these crimes fall within the field of criminology, the branch of organised crime.

Theoretical Construction

To establish a general theory that can simulates the crimes of agent parties in Iraq, various approved hypotheses were tested. And each hypothesis was validated through its actual field noticing of the committed crimes. This route enabled the extraction of the theory statement texts theoretically and logically to have the general concept of the theory and to deduce its theoretical laws.

The First Hypothesis:

Often agent parties of a foreigner appear after the collapse or fall of the political system by the foreign occupation and the uprooting of the ruling party.

The confirmation of this hypothesis stems from what the US Governor of Iraq (Paul Bremer) said to the new ambassador to Iraq (Negro Ponte): that the US government preferred weak, corrupt, and fraudulent elements who do not disclose what they want and pretend to be kind, simple, pious, skilled in the art of fraud and cunning, who are good at making words and are intellectually empty and failed Politically. They know with certainty that they are isolated from the people; they do not receive any appreciation or consideration on the part of the citizens. They believe that defrauding people is wit, and engage in procrastinating promises, seizing the assets of others, and usurping the property of the citizen as spoils of war. They are charlatans and hypocrites, the turban wearers, the tramps, and the secular, strutting, alike, and their appetites are open to everything related to public funds, treasures, and the acquisition of palaces. [Al Omer. 2016. p. 376].

The Second Hypothesis:

The external conflict often leads to internal solidarity for the sake of unity and cohesion of the group against external aggression.

This is what was confirmed by the contemporary American sociologist (Lewis Coser) in his theory called (Conflict positives), where he said: The external conflict between groups leads to internal solidarity for the joint group in the conflict process, which in turn leads to the suppression of every internal movement or implicit conflict (within the group) The one). [Al Omer 1982. p. 43). This theory was also explained by Ibn Khaldun, who stated that the conflict between tribes leads to internal solidarity - within the same tribe in order to preserve its unity. [Al Omer. 1982. p. 40]. However, this theory was not true for the Iraqi society when America occupied it in 2003, as there was disintegration and bloody conflicts between the components of Iraqi society (between the Shiite sect and the Sunni community, and between the Kurds and Arabs) although they are living within one society and they are in front of an invader and a foreign occupier. In this aspect, the Peshmerga helped the American army to invade Iraq, and the Iraqi refugees in Iran contributed to fighting the Iraqi army and assisting the American army. There was no national unity or social unity, but rather a rupture has occurred between its factions, and fatal clashes and conflicts erupted between them. Therefore, not every external conflict leads to internal solidarity for the group in conflict with the external enemy, but rather the opposite happens, especially with the help of the external enemy to overthrow the ruler, to wrestle with his followers and his inner circle, so that internal disintegration takes place, and the group is divided into conflicting factions among themselves, and the foreigner helps to dismantle it. This is what happened in Iraqi society after 2003, and this is a reversal of the theory of Lewis Coser and Ibn Khaldun in the theory of the positives of the conflict.

The Third Hypothesis:

The appropriation of three main authorities (sectarian, political, and financial) with one hand, which often leads to not exercising them fairly and responsibly.

This appropriation took place in Iraq and lasted for seventeen-odd years in the hands of sectarian and tribal parties, which led to their practice of moody arbitrariness that served the parties rather than serving the society but damaging it and made it suffer from injustice, extortion, corruption, thereby neglecting the reconstruction of the country and taking care of its people and investing its human resources in a time of need for education, health, work, security, and safety. In this respect, they exploited the feelings and sentiments of the poor, the illiterate and the commoners to serve the ruling class in the elections without providing them with any services, focusing on concluding contracts, deals and foreign trade and taking commissions from them in every ministry while deceiving the people with a policy loyal to and serving Iran instead of Iraq. The confiscation of the three authorities and placing them in one hand does not make them balanced, straight, and fair in their performance, especially when they are in the hand of those who are deprived of them, persecuted and destitute, who suffer from the passion living and are ignorant of religious and cultural knowledge. They will definitely misuse these authorities and are confused in their behaviour, and they become perverted and criminal in the right of the individuals who are subject to them. This is how the Shiite parties in Iraq were before they came to rule Iraq before 2003. They were chased by the former regime and were homeless in parts of the world. They have no previous experience in exercising power, live on the social aids of western governments who have resorted to them. They are socially submerged that do not have money, influence, and power, and suddenly by chance, they possessed spiritual-sectarian power and political power that they were deprived of. They did not have competence and experience in any authority, while suddenly, they possessed financial authority in a country rich in money and multi-religious denominations that suffers from the dominance of the American occupation. These parties were not able to absorb the three authorities with one hand at a one time. They abused them first, especially since it is for the first time in history that they govern Iraq. Therefore, they abused Iraqi society. They were and are tyrannical in ruling Iraq and exaggerated their domination and abused other sects, and plundered the wealth of Iraq without feeling shame or disgraced. They could not believe that all this wealth, powers, and authorities together in their hand. They were worried about losing everything from their hand, so they suppressed, killed, and plundered the money of everyone standing in their way. These authorities (spiritual, political, and financial) made them become criminals against a people exhausted by wars, economic blockades, totalitarian rule, and foreign occupation. They took unjustified revenge with all their strength from people and plundered their money instead of being trustworthy. They were not fair in their judgment, and they did not possess the patriotic spirit over their country. Besides that, they did not preserve the teachings of their sect, so they distorted the sectarian teachings in their favour, plundered the money entrusted to them, violated the laws of the country they govern. They corrupted the principles, the moral and normative standardised measures that society relied on, so they were anti-social parties, robbers of public funds, undermined customary controls, agents of the foreigner who was hostile to Iraq and coveted his wealth and experiences, and traitors to Iraq. Therefore despotism, recklessness and corruption of all kinds became characteristics of the Shiite parties that prevailed in Iraq for more than seventeen odd years. This anomaly was not experienced by Iraq before.

Pre-American occupation in 2003, the political authority was in the hand of professional politicians who were very competent decision-makers, while sectarian power was in the hands of the clergy, the judiciary was in the hands of the judiciary men, and the financial authority was in the hands of the economists, and the administrative power was in the hands of those with experience in managing all activities and functions of the country. However, these authorities have been abducted by Shiite parties simultaneously as one category. All members of these parties, without exception, have limited intelligence, lacking administrative experience and political leadership. They were financially poor and unknown socially. They neither have a past nor an honourable historical background in the history of Iraqi society. They are a group of criminal gangs rather than political parties as well as being terrorist groups stigmatised with violence, crime, and hostility to Iraq. This is the matter that has attracted the enemies of Iraq, such as Iran, America, and Israel, to depend on these traitors' parties in sabotaging and destroying the social structure, stealing its wealth, and assassinating its intellectuals, scholars, and military leaders. It is, therefore, a valid statement to say: the gathering of three main authorities with one hand does not make them clean, honest, fair, balanced, and merciful, but oppressive, terrifying, and thieves without accountability. And since they are the foremost command, they turned into the plunderers, donors, oppressors, and outcasts.

As for the Sunni parties, they did not possess these three authorities but rather the sectarian authority of the Sunni community through the Endowment Department. It did not have the political or financial authority because it lost them due to its lack of appreciation of the state of occupation of Iraq, and it is exaggerating its power without cooperation with other political components. As for the Kurdish parties, they possessed four authorities simultaneously, which are the Kurdish national (not sectarianism), tribal, political, and financial authorities. The possession of several authorities with one hand at one time, while they are not qualified, is considered extremely dangerous. On top of that, they are still representing a social minority in Iraq. Their ignorance in the administration of the country created an imbalance in their political balance. They turned from poor people to emperors, from limited education to businessmen, and from persecuted to oppressors for a society of multiple religious, ethnic, political, and tribal affiliations, and occupied by a foreigner and greedy for neighbouring countries who wanted to take revenge and plunder its wealth. These parties were the best carriers rode by the Americans, Iranians, and Israelis. Therefore, Iraqi society has paid a heavy price on all levels; human, financial, geographical, moral, religious, security and military. They converted it into a permissible society subject to extortion and money laundering.

These parties did not pay any attention to reforming what had been corrupted by wars, the totalitarian regime, and the occupation, nor did they build a new Iraq, nor did they save its people from illiteracy, unemployment, disease, and poverty. On the contrary, they increased illiteracy, unemployment, poverty, and disease and turned it into a society suffering from many diseases and ignorance. These three authorities made them human monsters that did not know mercy, humanity, honesty, integrity, responsibility, and patriotism. They offended the principles of the Jaafari sect and tribal fanaticism (for the Kurds) and the Hanafi school (for the Sunni endowment). The loose money without monitor, the absent law, absolute and primitive sectarian power among the Shiites and Sunnis were exploited by the usurpers of the three authorities, so they became avenges of all who stand in front of them and hold them accountable and demand their rights. Thus, the gap has become large between these parties and the general public and a national gap between those who lack them and their claimants, a gap between the new rich class, the middle class and the lower class. The result was sectarianism between Sunnis and Shiites, a tribal gap between the Barzani's, the Talabani, and Kurdish tribes, a generational gap between the conscious youth and the holders of the three and four authorities. Also, a cultural gap between the intellectuals and the claimants of culture and an institutional gap between the deep state and the investors. They are fabricated parties - tailored to serve their members, not the society, concerned only with power and control, and has no national social goals. They use coercive and compulsory control in conjunction with financial control, combined with sectarian and tribal control that use material rewards for their members. They practised feudal administration, so they were groups that exploit individuals who did not possess political awareness and historical memory of Iraqis, whether they were Shiites, Sunnis, or Kurds, to deceive them with mirage and dreamy goals that they did not implement but raised slogans to deceive the innocent people. There were no changes through reform or revival, but rather wide and deep gaps between the components of Iraqi society (between sects, tribes, generations, and governorates). The authority of the Shiite, Sunni and Kurdish parties was not socially acceptable and did not represent legitimacy. They did not obtain the acceptance of the followers in granting them the right to lead because it was instated to rule by the American occupier and the support of the Iranian government. Therefore, there was a rape of the authorities, and they were and are illegal authorities that do not have the knowledge and experience in their exercise and management. These authorities were oppressive, plunderer, and repressive, hence unacceptable to Iraqi society with all its components. In light of this, the following happened: -

1. Growing political, financial, and administrative corruption.

2. Flabbiness of the state organisations by disguised unemployment and the deep state.

3. Widening gap between the ruling parties and the general population of Iraqis.

4. High standard of living and its costs.

5. High rate of unemployment and poverty.

6. Confiscation of authoritarian positions by the leaders of the parties.

All of this suffering led to the indignation and grumbling of the Iraqi society, expressing it with the following: -

1. The continuing acts of protest against government terrorism, its corruption, its sabotage, its sectarian partisanship, and intolerance against the Sunnis.

2. The growing number of social ammunitions affected by the corruption of the parties.

3. Organising mature Shiite and Kurdish youth movements aware of what is happening to them and around them.

4.   Exploiting the political crises faced by the ruling parties in order to destabilise the corners of political harmony.

The Fourth Hypothesis:

This hypothesis states: that the agents' parties' crimes against major government institutions with huge financial returns that are devoted to building public facilities and commit themselves to contracts with companies that are in trade with the opponents of the previous state are often varied.

Ahmad Hadi proved this hypothesis in his article tagged (20 Corruption Cases How 500 billion were lost). These crimes are: -

1.   Explosive Detection Devices: Iraq imported in 2007 about six thousand explosive detection devices (sonar) at the cost of $200 million, after which it became clear that corrupted officials made a deal in which they earned millions of dollars by purchasing counterfeit devices that caused the deaths of thousands of Iraqis.

2.   Currency Auction: Official data stated that the Central Bank of Iraq sold nearly $312 billion through its auction to sell the currency since its inception, as 80% of those sums were leaked outside Iraq.

3.   50 Thousand Fictitious Personnel: On 30th September 2014, Prime Minister Haider Al-Abadi

revealed at the time that there were fifty thousand fictitious employees in the Ministry of Defence receiving salaries under fake names.

4. The Canadian Civil Aircraft Deal: Iraq bought in May 2008 (6) Canadian C5300 aircraft at double prices exceeding their real value by $277 million, after which the Iraqi government decided to sell them to a Canadian company at a value less than their price by 70%, as the aircraft were unsuitable for the narrow Iraqi airspace and could accommodate only 70 people.

5. Arms' Deals: Iraq lost billions of dollars as a result of arms deals with Russia and America, amounting to $150 billion. A large proportion of these funds went into the pockets of those involved in the deals in exchange for the poor quality of these deals and the preference for one side over another.

6. Minister of 9 Corruption Cases: The Integrity Commission associated with the Iraqi Parliament revealed that former Trade Minister Abdul Falah Al-Sudani is prosecuted for at least 9 corruption cases. He was sentenced in absentia to imprisonment in cases of damage to public money related to violations in the import of foodstuffs, and the security authorities received 25th January 2012. Al-Sudani

was arrested by the International Interpol, but he was released with a general amnesty.

7. School Structures: Former Minister of Education Khudhair Khuzaie in the government of Prime Minister Nuri Al-Maliki granted an Iranian company in 2008 a project to construct 200 schools of steel structures at the cost of ID280 billion ($232.7 million). The project has not been implemented so far due to their disagreements over the money with the Iraqi contractors, who numbered 18, most of whom fled Iraq.

8. Electricity, $29 billion: The volume of what was spent on the electricity sector in Iraq from 2006 until 2018 is estimated at $28 billion, according to an official report of the Iraqi Integrity Commission, while Iraqis suffered until last summer from hours of interruption of up to 18 hours per day.

9. Spoiled Biscuits: The story began when the journalist Hanan Al-Kiswani published in the Jordanian newspaper Al-Ghad a photo-backed investigation of an expired, spoiled shipment in September 2013, and it was extended to two additional years until 2015 to be exported to Iraq where it was distributed to schools despite being expired and became unfit for human consumption.

10. $100 billion in ISIS fire: Prime Minister Haider Al-Abadi estimated the cost of economic losses during 3 years of the Islamic State's control over vast areas in Iraq at more than $100 billion, while the authorities are still stalling the investigation file into the fall of Mosul despite the issuance of a final report on a committee assigned by parliament to investigate that condemned former Prime Minister Nuri Al-Maliki, former Mosul Governor Atheel Al-Najafi, military and security leaders, as well as officers in Mosul's local police.

11. The Looting of 121 Banks: ISIS also seized 121 governmental and other private sector banks in Nineveh, Kirkuk, Salah Al-Din and Anbar governorates, demonstrating its control over those governorates in 2014, during which it acquired about $1.0 billion. The funds obtained by ISIS as a result of selling oil are estimated at about $2 billion annually.

12. ID7.0 billion Sank: The most recent statement of the Central Bank Governor, Ali Al-Alaq, during his hosting from Parliament on 13th September 2018, that the safes of the Rafidain Bank were exposed to rainwater leakage and caused the damage of ID 7.0 billion.

13. Merge Officers - Sale of Military Ranks: Merge officers is a common term in Iraq in the post-2003 period of Former Prime Minister Nouri Al-Maliki, where traitors and relatives of the traitors are granted military ranks while they have no military training or military qualification.

14. The "Una Oil" scandal: An investigative investigation conducted by the "Febfax Media" and "Huffington Post" websites revealed the "involvement" of the former Minister of Higher Education and Scientific Research, Hussein Al-Shahristani, and other Iraqi officials, in a corruption scandal related to oil contracts, while He was known in the media as the "scandal of Unoil". The investigation talks about tens of billions of dollars that went into the pockets of the dealers.

15. Seizing State Real Estate: After the fall of Saddam Hussein's regime in 2003, political figures, officials and parties seized land, headquarters and buildings owned by the state in most areas of the capital. The price of one building is estimated at more than one million dollars, while the responsible authorities could not ask for these real estates, benefit from it or take it away from those in control of it.

16. Internet Smuggling: Internet smuggling in Iraq costs the state huge sums, estimated at $1.0 million a

month, according to the latest statement of the Integrity Commission that, besides the control of parties over this vital sector through companies and offices, it was proved that they were involved in these operations.

17. School Curricula: The printing of school curricula that has changed several times during the past years, according to the moods of the ministers who took charge of the ministry, costs millions of dollars, as these curricula are printed outside Iraq, while dozens of current and former officials were involved in these deals. In addition to that, there was a great negative impact of those changes to curricular content.

18. The Resources of the Ministries ... the Parties' Venues: Most of the state's parties have relied, in financing their projects, on the resources of the ministries that are controlled by officials belonging to those parties, as most of the ministries 'resources and allocations are allocated to finance these projects and electoral campaigns, and to pay the salaries of workers in the party's institutions, especially the media institutions.

19. Officials' Salaries ... Protections and Advisors: The salaries and allowances of officials in Iraq greatly exceed the level of officials' salaries in the countries of the region, as those salaries cost millions of dollars

and overburdened the Iraqi state over the past years, while the number of protections for senior officials in the state reached 25 thousand guards each of whom charges about $1500.

20.   Oil Smuggling: The major share of corruption was the share of oil smuggling operations, which cost Iraq more than $90 billion in 5 years, involving parties and influential figures in the central government and the Kurdistan Regional-Government. [https://ultrairaq.ultrasawt.com]

The Fifth Hypothesis:

The men of agents' parties often transfer their thefts and embezzlement to their personal bank accounts in several foreign countries to fortify themselves financially in the event they are removed from power.

This hypothetical text was confirmed by US President Donald Trump, who stated that the assets of Iraqi politicians amounted to $553 billion that were collected and seized from oil and weapons deals, corruption, and money laundering operations, from Iraq's wealth that the Iraqis did not benefit from, such as: -

1.   Nuri Al-Maliki, his balance in America's banks is $66 billion.

2.   Jalal Talabani, the former president of Iraq, has $31 billion in US banks.

3.   Bahaa Al-Araji, Former Deputy Prime Minister, $37 billion.

4.   Baqir Al-Zubaidi, former minister, $30 billion.

5.   Rafi'a Al-Issawi, a former (Sunni) minister, $29 billion.

6.   Osama Al-Najafi, former Speaker of Parliament (Sunni), $28 billion.

7.   Masoud Barzani, president of the Kurdistan region (Kurdish), $59 billion.

8.   Hoshyar Zebari, former (Kurdish) foreign minister, $21 billion.

9.   Adnan Al-Asadi $25 billion.

10. Saleh Al-Mutlaq (Sunni) $28 billion with investments, assets and real estate in Saudi Arabia and Turkey.

11. Muhammad Al-Darraji $19 billion.

12. Saadoun Al-Dulaimi (Sunni) $18 billion.

13. Farouk Al-Araji $6 billion.

14. Haider Al-Abadi $17 billion.

15. Muhammad Al-Karbouli (Sunni) $20 billion.

16. Ahmed Nouri Al-Maliki, $14 billion.

17. Tariq Najm, $7 billion.

18. Ali Al-Alaq $19 billion.

19. Ali Al-Yasiri $12 billion.

20. Hassan Al-Anbari $7 billion.

21.   Ayad Allawi, $35 billion, has apartments in Al Dakhliya roundabout in Jordan and Britain, as well as companies, contracting and small production plants.

22.   Hussain Al-Shahristani, $15 billion, with oil investments.

23.   Nechirvan Barzani (Kurdish) $12 billion.

24.   Qobad Talabani (Kurdish), representing the Kurdistan region in America, $7 billion.

25.   Hiro Khan, the wife of Talabani (Kurdish), has 9 billion dollars, with gold coins, bonds and palaces in Sulaymaniyah and Erbil.

26.   Abbas Al-Bayati $11 billion.

27.   Hassan Al-Sunaid, $8 billion.

28.   Adel Abdul Mahdi $31 billion

No one of them possessed anything before the occupation. They were homeless scattered in parts of the world who lived on the aid of foreign governments from social security. They were unemployed in those countries because of their incompetence and their scientific and professional qualification, and through the rule of their parties (traitors' parties) in Iraq, they became billionaires.

However, the ownership of Ali Al-Sistani, the top cleric reference for Shiite, until 2006 was only $3 billion, but his annual income from the proceeds of the fifth is $500-$700 million. Donald Rumsfeld, the former US Secretary of

Defence, revealed in his memoirs that his country paid the Shiite reference cleric in Iraq Ali Al-Sistani $200 million to issue a fatwa prohibiting the Shiites from fighting the Americans or forming popular resistance against the American occupation in order to facilitate the falling of Iraq in the hands of the occupying power. As for Sistani's son-in-law Mortadha Kashmiri, he bought a villa in London for $6 million, and his second son-in-law, Jawad Shahristani, did the same and bought a villa in London for $4 million. As for Al-Sistani's daughter, she bought an additional third villa in London for about $2 million. The young Shiite cleric, Ammar Al-Hakim, however, owns a fortune of 33 million dollars in the form of funds and investments in oil companies and real estate in Iran, Lebanon, London, the Emirates, Kuwait, and Saudi Arabia. He also owns various giant transportation companies inside and outside Iraq. As for the young Muqtada Al-Sadr, his wealth is $2 billion, with assets, properties and companies in Lebanon, Iran, and Turkey.

The Sixth Hypothesis:

This hypothesis states that the victim of the foreign agents' parties ruling often suffers psychological and social damage as a result of that judgment.

The victim here is the entire Iraqi society, with all its sects and spectrums, because the perpetrator does not have a patriotic relationship with the society but is rather a vehicle and an agent of the foreign government that is avenging him, which is Iran and America, such as:-

1. Psychological Depression: the rate of psychological depression in Iraq has reached 45%. Most of it is due to security turmoil and lack of safety due to bombings, assassinations, sectarian conflict, high levels of poverty and unemployment among university graduates, widespread bribery, extortion, abuse of agent parties' men, and the parties' militias control of social and political life.

2. The Suicide: In 2018, 50 people aged between 17 and 23 years committed suicide in the Dyala governorate, and there are 23 males who committed suicide by shooting, burning, and falling from higher distances. As for the females, there were 23 cases of suicide by burning, hanging, and cutting a vein. Between 2003 and 2013, more than 1,500 suicides appeared, and between 2015-2017, there were 3,000 suicides, with Theeqar governorate at the forefront, followed by Dyala, then Nineveh, Baghdad, and Basra. [www.basnews.com]

3. Sectarian Violence: a group of acts of violence, mass killings and bombings targeting residential or civilian gatherings, such as markets and residential neighbourhoods in predominantly Sunni or Shiite areas, with the aim of revenge or sectarian

liquidation based on a fanatical sectarian ideology have become commonplace. A quarter of a million Iraqis have fled because of sectarian violence, in which dozens of Sunnis and Shiites are killed daily. Mosques belonging to Shiites and Sunnis are attacked with car bombs in different neighbourhoods of Baghdad and other governorates. Mass killings have happened on a sectarian basis targeting Sunnis and Shiites, not to mention assassinations in Basra and sectarian displacement.

4. Drug Abuse: After 2003, drug abuse became common, and it is sold on the sidewalks, so that one out of every ten people between the ages of 18-30 years old became addicted, and one out of every three members of the security forces uses some sort of a drug. The statistics of the National Commission for Drug Control stated that the number of armed addicts reached 16,000, including more than a thousand children between the age of 14-15 years old in Baghdad due to unemployment, depression, fear of the future and anxiety. Simply, Iraq became a station for drug cultivation and manufacture.

5. Unemployment: the unemployment among Iraqi youth exceeds 22.6% for university graduates and holders of higher degrees due to mismanagement, widespread corruption, and the lack of real plans to

revive the economy. In addition, the ruling parties do not open the way to foreign investments, exercise political quotas on available jobs, and have the influx of foreign workers of various nationalities.

6. Social Phobia and Psychological Disorders: There are 20% of Iraqis suffering from mental disorders [www.almaalomah.com] because of fear and constant and intense anxiety about some social situations and a belief in mistrust, humiliation, and tension. It is a chronic mental illness that affects human feelings and behaviour as well as changes the way he speaks or behaves in social interaction, and fear of communicating with strangers whom he meets for the first time, plus the fear of their judgments that are causing embarrassment or ridicule because of difficulty in communicating and speaking or doing things and tasks with a flickering voice.

7. Sexual Harassment: According to the BBC and the Arab Barometer poll, men in Iraq are exposed to sexual harassment more than women in public places, with a percentage of 20% for men and 17% for women. Female employees and women workers in the private sector, female students and passers-by in the commercial markets are subject to harassment. Even women visitors to government departments are

harassed before completing their cases, especially in institutions such as social care from where the widow and divorced obtain their salary. It highlights the inferior view of women. Harassers are both from high-ranking positions on the career ladder and range from the youngest officials to the general directors, particularly when it comes to promote and send them abroad after an invitation or to attend a conference. The state of sexual harassment appeared intensely after the protests that erupted in October 2019, when the militias became dominant as the sectarian conflicts that Iraq has lived through contributed to the increase in the number of widows and orphans and pushing women to the labour market in complex circumstances. And it was aggravated by the absence of national government as the women became prey to persecution and extortion by the bosses of work. And even some clerics exploit the poverty of women and bargain with them in exchange for their sexual desires for giving them what they need, which means the harassment is within the work environment and the society in general.

8. Homosexuals: openness and freedom after 2003 with Muqtada Al-Sadr's call to end violence against homosexuals in July 2016, it has become a rampant phenomenon, but it is silent on it. Homosexuals have

openly defined themselves on some pages spread on social media, so they are subject to kidnapping and rape.

9. Non-standardized Replaced the Normative: The Non-standardised and non-traditional rules dominated the interactions and relationships of Iraqis with ruling agents' parties due to their practices with government institutions and with the people in behaviour contrary to the orthodox standards that prevailed in Iraq before their rule. They turned the forbidden into permissible, the unreasonable into the reasonable, integrity became repugnant, and theft into art, forgery into cleverness, bribery into gratuity, plunder into a window of opportunity, betrayal into an interest, and employment into friendship. This non-standardisation led to the spread of moral, political, and financial corruption, which weakened the cognitive, social controls in Iraqi society.

The Seventh Hypothesis:

Often the money laundering of embezzled funds by politicians and security leaders in gambling halls and luxury restaurants plays an important role in spreading corruption in the process of its recycling via spending and investment.

The agents' parties practised financial and political corruption in stealing public money. They are laundering and recycling it through their investments in order to give legal legitimacy for the purpose of possessing, disposing of, depositing, or transferring it in the form of a fake import by those who have influence commensurate with the level of their position. The influential are transferring the stolen money out of Iraq while those who are less powerful are recycling their stealing inside. In view of this, the authorities ignore the exorbitant and rapid wealth of many politicians as well as unknown merchants who quickly turn into masters in the labour market, taking advantage of the security forces with weak government oversight agencies and their lack of experience. Money laundering has weakened the national income through depletion of capital, its flight to abroad and monetary instability. The phenomenon of money laundering is escalating in Iraq, in line with the spread of drug trade, gambling and prostitution halls, the rise in human trafficking crimes and the rampant financial corruption in all state institutions. The corrupt sources of funds are mainly bank robberies and the smuggling of valuable antiquities to sell them on global markets. In addition to their plundering of oil and its derivatives, smuggling of machinery, tools, equipment, and factories abroad, they found that industrial and commercial fraud via establishing fake projects and services are extra good sources of funds for their corruption. Instead of penalising such corruption, the Iraqi judiciary supported the corrupt by closing 2,500 money laundering cases. They were closed by an Iraqi judge who was rewarded for his corruption support and given money and six-month enjoyment leaves that he spent in Lebanon.

Ruling of the Tails of Shiite Parties
(Donor Thieves)

Political and religious parties are considered by Sociologists to be among the formal organisations that mediate between the people and the government in modern urban and industrial societies. They convey the suffering, demands, and needs of society to the government in a formal and logical defence of them and inform statesmen of what is happening in the collective base popular base of problems and crises. In effect, the formulation of parties had started as a need and in response to the weakness of the monitoring system, the growth of specialisations, the presence of the compound and complex social organisations in construction and functions, the emergence of the phenomenon of uniqueness as a result of industrialisation, and the emergence of the opponent trend that highlighted the central need within the organisation. And due to the emergence of the dispossession phenomenon at that time, secondary organisations were crystallised, currently known as parties to mediate a direct contact with the government and to form a link between the masses and the ruling authority.

But what happened in Iraqi society after the American invasion of Iraq in 2003 and the collapse of the Baath state, religious parties with a sectarian religious character crystallised that took power for a period that lasted for more than seventeen years. They did not have an ideological doctrine, a strategy to build Iraq, or even to reform it after the foreign wars destroyed most of its infrastructure, structural, security and military superstructure. Groups with greedy interests emerged that have no respect socially, politically, intellectually, and religiously, who dream of a state similar to that of the Iranian Guide which incubated them when they were opposing Saddam regime, bypassing the status of being agents to Iran as they were fighting alongside it against Iraq in the eight-year war, such as Muhammad Baqir Al-Hakim, Hadi Al-Ameri, Al-Maliki and the Da'wa Party. When the Da'wa Party took power in Iraq from 2006 to 2018, it was a disastrous experience by all standards that brought Iraq closer to the status of a failed state, during which the administrative, financial, and moral corruption spread. The most dangerous phase was during the presidency of the party's secretary-general, Nuri Al-Maliki, who became the prime minister from 2006 to 2014. During this period, a trillion dollars disappeared without leaving any positive impact in improving the economic and social conditions and upgrading the infrastructure that has worn out, eroded, and nullified in many regions. In order to scrutinise the foregoing, it can be stated that the Shiite parties have exploited the simplicity of thinking of the Shiite masses in southern and central Iraq by justifying their hegemony over the ruling system with the following:

1. Their claim of the historical injustice that occurred against the Shiites throughout the life of modern Iraq.

2. Their exclusion from the ruling.

3. The rule of the Sunnis, who are the minority.

4. The right of the Shiites to rule Iraq as they are the majority of the population.

5. Them being the only ones who defied and confronted Saddam's regime.

It is worth mentioning in this context that the Shiite, Sunni, and Kurdish parties have formed armed militias, armies, and secret prisons not to defend themselves from the foreigner but to kill, imprison and torture any Iraqi who objects to their rule. Such actions do not represent the official intermediary organisations between the people and the government, but rather for the forced domination of the people for the sake of intimidation to continue their ruling of Iraq and to destroy everything that benefits and serves society. They caused agony, pain, and death of many Iraqis. Therefore, they plundered Iraqi wealth and handed it over to Iran in exchange for its support for their rule. They were not more than tails for the Iranian government to ride them whenever it needed and use them as a force of revenge against the Iraqis and plundering their wealth. Thus, Iraq is ruled by Iraqi Shiites who were and are tails and agents to the Iranian government as Iraqi of Persian non-Arab origins to practice revenge and retaliate against them more than broadcasting their call for Guardianship of the Jurist.

Most of the Iraqis martyred in the war with Iran were killed at the hand of these traitors, and many more were disabled. In addition, the Iranian are using these tails to plunder the financial coffers of Iraq, which cost the Iraqi government more than the cost of its war with Iran. It is not wrong, then, to state that the Iranian government rode those tails who have no national affiliation, neither have loyalty to their Shiite sect nor ethical principles. In addition to their lack of knowledge of the art of running the country, they are traitors bragging and flaunting the rulers of Iran. Rather, they are bragging and fawning to the rulers of Iran, so they were uglier than the American colonial rule over Iraq.

This is a new method of modern colonialism that uses the country's mercenaries (the tails), including the lowly, the homeless, those with criminal precedents, the outcasts, and the greedy, to steal public and private money. In order to clarify what mentioned earlier, we say: What did the Shiites of Iraq benefit from the rule of the parties that exercised power in their name and made their leadership and beliefs slogans for them and derived from their historical symbols and religious sanctities powers that raised their leaders above the rank of ordinary people? We say that during its leadership of the state, of the Shiites, or of the Iraqis, it did not accomplish anything that could relate to the component that we consider its main incubator, as it did not build or establish projects for modern development. It rather linked Iraq to the Iranian sphere of influence and made it an arena for settling its accounts against its regional and international opponents, chief among them the United States. This means that they were neither Iraqi national parties nor intermediary organisations between the Iraqis and the government. Rather, they were Shiite sectarian interest-based organisations with a Persian and not an Arab reference that wore the dress of politics ostensibly, and they were tails that rode by the Iranian government with the aim of:

1. Retaliation against the Iraqis without discrimination among them. They killed the Arab Shiites and the Sunnis due to the historical hostility and the war with them and the destruction of its war machine.

2. Displacement of many of them.

3. Plundering its financial wealth, treasuries, and natural resources (oil and natural water).

4. Spreading moral corruption in the use of drug cultivation, which the Iraqis did not know before.

5. The formation of military and security institutions loyal to Iran.

6. Making Iraq a popular market for Iranian goods and articles.

7. Transforming Iraqi society from the civilised stage to the pre-industrial stage.

8.   Expanding the problem of unemployment among Iraqi youth.

9.   Distorting Shiite teachings to serve disgusting Iranian purposes.

10.   The establishment of the deep state that emerged due to the fragility and weakness of the state with the emergence of political and religious parties and militias that have no loyalty to Iraq. These reasons have created mafias and corruption gangs within the state, it is a deep state but in a negative way that works contrary to what the regular state does ... These parties fought for power as they came to serve Iran and personal interests not to serve and remain a strong state, it is cancer in the body of Iraq, that is, the domination of mafias that facilitate matters Party members in the event they need plunder, smuggling, embezzlement, and control of ministries, especially the interior, passports, the army, and residency, as there are 75% of state matters placed by the parties within the official institutions, and Iran was a major factor in forming the deep state in Iraq through the Iraqi parties loyal to it and their militias.

11.   Every party has now a jurist to justify the stealing to the followers of the party and legitimise the use of what they acquired from state property, so it is easy for ruin to happen and its area to expand. This is

something that only the gullible and idiots can do to fool the naive who believe in them.

12.   The stupid, naive, and sterile behaviour is manifested in that the tails of Iran have combined the religious pattern with the political system while they are different in motives and goals. The first is dominated by strong human and moral standards, and the second is dominated by self-interest and the current desires, which fluctuates between circumstantial goals and personal motives. Whereas the tails were not established by religious or political upbringing, and they found themselves in positions of political power to delude the Iraqi Shiites that they are their saviours and defenders of their doctrine. The reality of their situation, however, is an embodiment of Iran, the historical enemy of Iraq who was able to curb their ambition, greed and to triumph over them. Now and with the role of its tails role, the suitable moment has come to confiscate Iraq's sanctities, wealth, and its ancient history. By all means, this combination will not continue because it is incompatible and antagonistic. No matter how violence, terror and foolishness are used on the Iraqis, the Shiite sect will return to its religious pattern, and professional politicians will come to occupy the political system without the need to exploit religious sentiment in its

politics. My purpose in this proposition is to emphasise that these parties do not represent official intermediary organisations. They are rather sectarian, armed factional groups hostile to the Iraqis without exception and a striking force in plundering Iraq's wealth and turning it to Iran to save its economy. Therefore, it has put forth falsehoods that have exploited the mob, the gossip, and the ignorant in religion, politics, and the illiterates, to deceive them and turn them into a reservoir to be utilised in electoral processes, Husseini funerals, and Shiite events, as well as in killing those who opposed it or throwing them into armed militias against anyone who objected to their rule. They were like poisonous snakes to bite and poison the Iraqis, and they are originally the tails and rides of the Iranian government in Iraq. They are similar to the organisations of the Catholic Church during the Middle Ages of the ecclesiastical and feudal rule. It is important to point out; what empowered the rule of those tails in Iraq is the application of the quota share system, which expresses a system for sharing wealth between parties and militias that have squeezed Iraq into sectarian sites. It acts as the cover-up of parties formed from the corrupt people, thieves, bandits, forgers, employers of precedents, and servants of foreigners, followers, loyalists, and agents.

These are the pro-Iranian tails from the Shiite parties, which are: -

1.	The leader of the Dawlat Al Qanoon coalition, Nouri Al-Maliki.

2.	The leader of the Badr Organization, Hadi Al-Ameri.

3.	The leader of the Asa'ib Ahl Al-Haq Movement, Qais Khazali.

4.	The leader of the Ataa' Movement, the head of the Popular Mobilization Authority and the National Security Adviser, Faleh Al-Fayyad.

5.	Al-Nujaba militia, the Imam Ali Brigades, the Sayyid Al-Shuhada' Brigades, Saraya Al-Khorasani, and the Hezbollah Brigades and Rabua'allah.

6.	Al Hikma Movement led by Ammar Al-Hakim

7.	Haider Al-Abadi, leader of the Nasr Coalition.

8.	Muqtada Al-Sadr, Al Salam Brigades, and his armed army.

9.	Al-Mukhtar Army.

10.	Brigades of Jihad W Al Bina'a.

11.	Al Mahdi Army of the Sadrist movement, which is largely made up of Shiites belonging to the former (Ba'athist) regime, declared repentance and organised on a sectarian basis for this trend.

12.	Abu Al-Fadil Al-Abbasi Armed Brigade.

13.   Al Fadhila Islamic Party.

Reviewing the activities of these parties and their militias, brigades, and military battalions makes one ascertain that there is no central national government that manages the affairs of the country but that every Shiite group has its own armed army as if it is fighting an enemy state. It became evident they do not obey the tolerant Shiite teachings, do not possess the Iraqi national feeling, and do not believe in Iraqi unity. Were there not in the history of modern Iraq any patriotic Shiite men who fought the British and the Americans, called for national unity and served Iraq and the Iraqis? Where do they apply their saying (The hand that performs ablution does not steal, did they not claim piety and religiosity?). They are no more than false Shiites. They are no more than false Shiites. Why did they not unite and build Iraq and show a wonderful national image in their faith and love for their country? Why did they race to steal their country's wealth? Why did they embrace the historical enemy to them and Iraq (the Magi Persians)? All these fake parties and armed militias proved on the ground they are against Iraq and Iraqis and are hostile to the Ja'fari sect and against Islam? Simply because they made great efforts to tear apart the national unity and insult Islam, and they asserted that they are terrorists and aggressive with the Iraqi people.

As for the motives of their division, it is due to the race in plundering, killing, and kidnapping everyone who wants to earn money and property from him. Why did they not fight the American forces in Iraq? And why did they not fight Israel, which they claim to be their enemy? This reveals that they mobilised for the illicit acquisition of state property and its border outlets and the taking of royalties from merchants and investors as they shared the sources of their thefts from Iraq's oil wealth, marketing it, selling currency, robbing banks, killing Sunnis, smuggling weapons and people, and cultivating drugs. What will the future Iraqi generations say, especially the Shiite youth who are aware and open to their people in this historical period that lasted more than seventeen years?

They stigmatised the Shiites of Iraq as the enemies of the Shiites and the enemies of the Ja'fari sect because they are murderers, thieves, saboteurs, and without any humanity. According to the interpretation of sociology, especially those of the functionalist constructivist theory, it is a condition that represents (functional impairment) for the theorist (Ernest Nickel), which he described as occurring when the goals of the regime did not help individuals to adapt to their goals and acquire them. This is what has happened in the sense that the Shiite parties and militias neither helped the Iraqis to adapt to the goals of the Shiite sect nor the ruling politician regime. They have planted fighting and civil war with them, stole their money, destabilised their nation, killed them, and imprisoned them.

By 2003, Saddam's regime was toppled, the party was uprooted, and the military and security institutions were dismantled. Could they not have rebuilt the ravaged Iraq by foreign wars? Did they not benefit and learnt a lesson from authoritarian rule and the exclusivity of power to adopt a national policy that unites Iraqis and gives them intellectual freedom and respect for the other opinion? Were they not supposed to preserve the wealth of Iraq that was plundered by the American invasion? Were they not required to conserve Iraq's oil and save its people after the United Nations imposed the economic blockade? Why did they not act as citizens of a free country? Why did they fall into the arms of Iran and America?

They have missed a rare opportunity to give a bright image to the Shiites of Iraq as they are, for the first time, taking over the rule of Iraq and rebuilding Iraq to be builders and saviours of Iraq. However, they carried out the same tyranny, arbitrariness and sectarian fanaticism that Saddam Hussein and his party did. They have subjected Iraqis to surveillance and accountability by the parties' economic committees, the deep state, special security agencies, secret prisons, the proliferation of weapons in the hands of militias, dwarfing the authority of the army and making the sect's men control the Iraqis just as the Ba'athists were controlling the

Iraqi people. There is no crime, then, in saying that for more than 1400 years, the Shiites of Iraq talk about oppression and tyranny and complain to the owner of the time (Al Mahdi) about the oppression of the rulers, and when they ruled, they presented the worst ruling model on the globe. Faced with these tyrannical, tyrannical contexts, it made Iraqis pity the rule of Saddam and his party, who died and did not have a house for him and his family to live in.

He achieved security and safety throughout his rule, built schools and hospitals, eliminated illiteracy, sent scientific scholarship abroad, received respect from the countries of the world, and Iraq prospered in its development and built an ideological army that defended the homeland for more than eight years and faced the latest lethal military weapons and broke the thorn of the Iranian army. The behaviour of the Iranian tails was, in fact, the behaviour of the mindless animals. I turn now to presenting the most prominent disasters brought about by the tails of parties that were mounted by the Iranian government, namely: -

1. The invasion of ISIS organisation of Iraq in the summer of 2014 and its occupation of nearly a third of its area in light of the inability of the military and security establishment to confront its fighters due to its decay and the infiltration of corruption and sectarianism into its ranks. Even the estimated number of the fictitious military employed affiliated

in it during the rule of Al-Maliki was more than fifty thousand individuals who were paid without any participation in the service.

2. The registration of fictitiously affiliated employees took place during Nuri Al-Maliki presidency of the government, which lasted for eight years. They were employees who received salaries and financial allocations without any presence of them, hence without doing any work in return for that. This phenomenon is widely spread in all institutions and agencies of the state, especially the army and police. Prime Minister Haider Al-Abadi revealed on 30th November 2014 the presence of more than fifty thousand officers and soldiers in four military divisions within this category, on which 500 million dollars are spent a month and have depleted the state's resources and affected the workflow. Also, there are 500 thousand fictitiously employed affiliated men in Kurdistan who receive their salaries from the Iraqi government.

3. These tails rode by the Iranian government have committed various crimes against the rights of Iraqis and their citizenship. Such crimes have lost the Iraqis their prestige and disrupted their institutions, including the judiciary, which is one of the most prominent symbols of the state's strength and its

ability to impose its justice and implement its laws on all its citizens without discrimination.

4. Deception of the impersonators of the religious reference authority in issuing deceptive and misleading religious fatwas that contradict the tolerant religious teachings, so that they permit the forbidden and forbade the permissible. In light of the gullibility and flattening of the religious knowledge of the ignorant majority who adhere to the religion in name and not knowing its truth, the impersonators of this characteristic have targeted the rabble and mob of the Shiites of Iraq to gain their support. Funny enough that in one of their deceiving fatwas, they permitted the theft of oil by considering it as the gift of God like the rain that falls on everyone without permission as long as it rains. Their justification was; since the oil is excavated from the ground that no one owns, it is a gift to all people and not for the government. This fraud was extended to state properties by considering their acquisition is permissible since there is no person who owns it, so according to this fatwa, they have the right to acquire it, not steal it. These fatwas are considered as real crimes that were committed by those who wear white and black turbans.

5.   The Shiite parties took advantage of the exhausted state of Iraq, which was suffering from the rule of the individual dictator, the economic siege that lasted thirteen years, and the collapse of its structural systems. They filled their pockets and earned money illegally and greedily and donated the stolen money to their Iranian riders in exchange for their support for their rule and supply of weapons to keep them in power.

6.   The Islamic political forces have relied on the revenues of the economic committees that are distributed according to a specific pattern that guarantees the provision of the necessary funding for special political projects. The economic committees belong to Shiite parties and militias, which are bodies that have been established in order to ensure the sustainability of financing the projects of parties and militias to reflect the partisan quota map. In their activity, these committees monitor the minister's performance and study all contracts and projects before they are awarded to determine the share percentage that the party should obtain from these contracts. One of the most famous ministers and committed to this work is Baqir Jabor Al-Zubaidi, who held the ministries portfolios for the ministries of reconstruction, housing, interior, finance, and

transportation. He is the most loyal to the economic committees responsible for following up the Supreme Islamic Council in the Iraqi ministries. Not only that, these committees also carry out money laundering operations around the world, collecting fees, transfer money and appoint employees in special grades.

7. The practice of assassinations of scholars, military men and patriotic activists.

8. After Nuri Al-Maliki assumed the duties of Commander-in-Chief of the Armed Forces in June 2006, he took advantage of the merger law and exploited it ugly with a handful of those around him. He singled out to grant ranks for those close to him and most of his relatives. He then conducted urgent arrangements for the members of the Da'wa Party, granting them military ranks without any right, as he ordered the promotion of 208 members to the rank of lieutenant-general and more than a thousand to the rank of major general. This is a huge crime against the Iraqi army and Iraq. These Shiite parties falsely used the peg of sectarianism, the Sunni menace, Wahhabism, fabricated Saudi conspiracies, and slogans to breathe the congestion of the Shiites of Iraq and justify their influence and corruption.

9. Iraqi ports have been subjected to Iranian infiltration through companies that are not registered with the Iraqi government but operating under cover of armed factions under the supervision of political parties that sponsor Iranian interests and pass oil deals, and tenders in favour of Iranian companies such as the Al-Fadhila Party led by Muhammad Al-Yaqoubi to infiltrate through its military forces called the (Brigade Shabab Al-Ressali) in several institutions in Basra. Iran has expanded its influence through Shiite political parties, and its Iraqi men (Iran tails) and militants have taken control of General Company for Iraqi Ports, Southern Oil Company, Oil Drilling and Exploration Company, Shuaiba Refinery, Petrochemical Company, Cement Company, Iron and Steel Company and Gas Company, which made Iran gains huge sums into its budget without the Iraqi government able to hold them accountable or put an end to this deviation because it carries out its economic activities with the protection of influential political parties, the most important of which are the Sa'eron alliance and the Dawlat Al-Qanoon coalition.

10. There are 22 land and sea border outlets with neighbouring countries, the most important of which are those with Iran. However, the Iranian Revolutionary Guard controls these ports through

their cooperation with the Popular Mobilisation factions.

11. Money laundering operations by smuggling hard currency from Iraq to Iran.

12. Cultivation and trafficking of drugs under the supervision and management of Iranians and Iraqi fighters to protect drug plantations on Iraqi lands in Jurf Al-Sakhar and in Babylon.

13. Emptied Iraq of its national content and put it on the path to sliding into the quagmire of sectarianism and penetrated the history of shared coexistence to control the financial and political capacity of Iraqi society.

14. The Shiite Endowment: It is a government within a government where the financial allocations of the Shiite and Sunni endowments mounted to ID813 billion, ID585 billion of which went to the Shiite endowment and ID284 billion to the Sunni endowment.

15. The fatwa of the unknown owner is the most dangerous religious motive to justify rampant corruption. It considers the state a legal entity that cannot be owned and cannot be traded within economic transactions. Likewise, the funds in the banks are regarded as money from unknown owners.

16.   Gambling halls resources are one of the resources of political and religious leaders. Believe it or not, roulette halls in Baghdad hotels are the most important economic resource for financing armed groups with a religious cover, as many political and religious leaders (militia) hide their financial resources through gambling halls that generate millions of dollars during one month in Palestine - Meridian Hotel. The halls administrator Hamza Al-Shammari manages the sex and prostitution networks through which money laundering operations are carried out for many political and religious figures whose assets are frozen inside and outside Iraq. This is indicating that Al-Shammari is linked to influential militia parties within the Popular Mobilization Authority whom some of its leaders provided security cover for him, as he is protected by the militia of Asa'ib and Al-Nujaba, Kataib Hezbollah, the Badr Organization, Ammar Al-Hakim and the Da'wa Party. All of them share Al-Shammari with the money earned by gambling halls, prostitution networks, drug trafficking and human trafficking that he runs, and red nights for leaders of the Popular Mobilization Forces, including clerics and leaders of parties affiliated with Iran, Hezbollah, and the Iranian Revolutionary Guard. They meet

with him and conclude political and commercial deals and the sale of ministerial and security positions. A million dollars are earned daily, which is a quarter, while the remainder of the amount is shared by Qais Al-Khazali, Ammar Al-Hakim, Nuri Al-Maliki, Hanan Al-Fatlawi, Akram Al-Kaabi, Abu Mahdi Al-Muhandis and Hadi Al-Amiri.

17. Side-lining the role of the Iraqi army and security forces by showing the militias that they are the only ones capable of carrying out any security task to protect the country. It means, it is a plan by the Iranian Revolutionary Guard that the Quds Force, the Iranian Revolutionary Guard wing, oversees, through militias, all human trafficking, prostitution, and drugs networks inside Iraq to implement a set of goals, including:

a. Bringing down influential political and security figures and businessmen who are not affiliated with Iran in this trap of prostitution networks and then recruiting them for the benefit of the Revolutionary Guards.

b. Obtaining hard currencies through these networks, gambling halls, and drug trafficking that go to Iran and its banks to support the terrorist activity of the Revolutionary Guard in the region.

Here, an urgent question arises: Are all the individuals involved in the militia members of the Ja`fari faith? The answer is 'absolutely no'. Rather, they are unemployed youth who come from the poor class and who was discharged from the army after its dismantling in 2003, so they had no source of livelihood in the face of the scarcity of self-employed and formal work opportunities and the high standard of living and its high costs. Therefore, there was no option other than engaging in these armed party militias supported by the Iranian government with the presence of enormous cash liquidity and extravagance in apparent consumption by the tails Iranian regime in Iraq that made them carry out the Iranian orders by the leaders of the parties in the name of the Shiites. In addition to supporting the official visual media outlets in exploiting the Shiite sadness in Ashura, the chest slapping, and the marching of condolences, which acted as collective influences for submission to these parties that give the impression that they are submissive to the Ja'fari doctrine. But they are, in fact, the agents of foreigners, the plunderers of Iraqi wealth indirectly by sparking a civil war between Sunnis and Shiites, bringing Al-Qaeda and ISIS to Iraq, and seizing the private and public property. All these factors have pushed the unemployed to turn into militia elements hostile to the Iraqis and loyal to Iran. On top of that, the support of the successive governments in power have received from the clerics, and the bearded men made them arrogant and imbalanced. As for the members of the Shiite parties, they are opportunists, precedents, bandits, fairness of the educated and forfeiters of school certificates. They do not have a patriotic feeling or political awareness but rather obtain a job opportunity by belonging to these parties that dominate state institutions. It is, therefore, not too much to say that there has been a gradual polarization that began with the Iranian regime's polarization of its tails in Iraq, who were then refugees in Iran. They were ignorant of the Ja`fari sectarian ideology and resent the members of the Iraqi Baathist regime that they wanted to revenge from it and its members. So, they met with the rulers of Iran in their revenge against the Iraqis and the plunder of its wealth while he was submitting under the American colonialism after they uprooted its institutions, dissolved its military and security institutions, destroyed its weapons and plundered its financial coffers. They took advantage of this collapse and carried out the orders of the Iranian government to kill Iraqi scholars, leaders, and officers, dismantle and steal factories, and destroy Sunni neighbourhoods and their cities. In other words, they were the enemies of Iraq more than the Iranians to it. Through the formation of economic committees, which are the authority authorized to disburse expenditures and allocated funds and conclude contracts in government institutions, from major contracts in the Ministry of Oil to the contract of the smallest cleaning company in an official department. Knowing that all contracts and expenditures are not subject to financial monitor and judicial oversight bodies because the parties and militias are above the authority of the law. They made banks and money transfer companies interfaces for the political parties that allow them to control the contracts and tenders. They also limit the infrastructure contracts to companies affiliated with political parties, then they worked to sell the positions of ministries, directorates and trafficking Out. It is clear that the tails of the Iranian regime who are represented by the autoreactive statemen, are associated with all parties and armed partisan militias. Their actions were not limited to financial embezzlement of state property but rather to its deliberate waste of spending on everything that is failed, fraudulent and corrupt. With this programmed approach, they entered Iran as a main partner in the Iraqi market, with financial returns amounting to about thirty billion dollars annually, which is an amount it earns from exporting its products to Iraq. And from energy supplies and construction and investment contracts that it acquires through facilities and exceptions provided by Iraq. Iran occupied or possessed eleven banks operating in Iraq independently. Iranian banks have also bought the share of six other Iraqi banks. The total funds of the Iranians in those banks amounted to more than seventy billion dollars. It reflects the absolute Iranian hegemony over the Iraqi economy, which was carried out by the tails of the Iranian government in Iraq. In order to be consistent with the foregoing, we say, the tails worked to bring about a moral downfall among those who belong to their parties and militias, so that they see the corruption as a normal behaviour which does not violate the honour and the social consideration. They supported their work by impersonating the religious reference authority in issuing false and misleading religious fatwas to thugs, mobs, commoners, and ignorant of religion. I called the actions of these impersonators (the crimes of those who wear white and black turbans among the clerics and sheikhs). As for the corruption of the tails, it represents crimes (white-collar as the American criminologist Dwayne Sutherland 1939 called it) that is non-violent crimes committed for financial motives by those with influence and the ruling class. Then there is the bloody criminality practised by the militia of religious parties against anyone who opposes or criticizes their party. It is a striking mechanism to the extent that the government fears them, does not hold them accountable, or punishes them for having advanced weapons that Iran is supplying them. In the context of the conversation, I must not overlook the existing fact that the tails and their Shiite parties have created corruption and the corrupt and continue to protect them, so they were the role models for their gangs and mercenaries in the ministries. They are the thieves of the

Kleptocrat state (those with thievery mania). The Sadrists own the Ministry of Health, the Badr Organization owns the Ministry of the Interior, and the Wisdom Movement owns the Ministry of Oil. They have made Iraq a swamp of corruption that suites them as they cannot live in a normal society free of corruption. This is right as their misbehaviour and corruption are the result of the complete absence of self-control, lack of conscience, principles and public oversight represented by the laws and regulations that the state ensure their implementation, and because corruption is linked to backwardness, ignorance, and irrational thinking. It is subject to a hierarchy, ranging from a lower grade to a minister grade, each of them practices corruption at the level of the position and the environment in which it is present at varying degrees more and more in the pivot points of institutions, transactions, and people's minds. There is another question that we raise in this context: since it is a Shiite government and the parties controlling it are also Shiite and supported by the Iranian government, so why do the members of these parties and their militias steal the state funds that they rule? And why do they have multiple armed militias while the military and security institutions are led by a Shiite government, which is their state? Who are they afraid of? It is clear that the Shiite government knows nothing but theft, fraud, forgery, and embezzlement, which is only carried out by thieves, ignorance of religion, immoral people, enemies of Iraqis and Iraq, and traitors and agents of foreigners. Moreover, as the government was their government, why did they not build and rebuild its edifices and distinguishing themselves among other religious sects to show that they came to build their state, bring to fruition their experiences and be proud of their achievements? So, they are not from the sons of Iraq, and they are not from the Ja'afari school of thought. Rather they are thieves, are vagabonds, and killers who do not understand human relations and have not experienced constructive activities. Therefore, it was the biggest mistake they have committed that lasted for more than seventeen years and did not stop destroying, corrupting, and plundering the money of their state!!! Their parties did not represent the intermediate organizations between the people and the government to act as a bridge that connects the suffering, problems, and needs of the people to the decision-makers, as in modern urban and industrial societies. But rather, they were a dependency for destruction and breaking up all the national forces and tears the Iraqi social fabric apart, robbing its wealth and smuggling it abroad in a donation to the chronic enemy of Iraq (Iran). These parties are humiliated criminal factions that their masters mount them because they feel social inferiority, political subservience, and financial greed. They are deprived of prestige, influence, and respect, whether in Iraq, Iran, or the rest of the world. They did not serve their sect and did not develop their cities, but rather impoverished them and pushed their unemployed people to turn into criminals against the Iraqi patriots. Their government, therefore, was a government of plunderers, donators, disgraceful and corrupt.

Finally, this is the organisation structure of this government:-

1. Tails of the regime

2. Mock political parties that are loyal to Iran and have no ideology, collective base, national identity, or political and administrative experience.

3. Armed party militias, whose authority is above the rule of law.

4. Political quotas (sectarian, partisan, and nationalist).

5. The deep state (economic bodies in every ministry affiliated with the parties).

6. Impersonating the personality of the religious reference authority, as every party has a religious authority that is permitting and forbidding according to the party's interest.

7. The inner circle of the political parties of the Shiite community.

8. The rabble, mobs and the common people in southern and central Iraq who are poor and destitute.

The Analysis and the Theorising for the Ruling of the Tails

Historical logic requires us to go back to the fundamental, historical, and sectarian causes of sabotage, destruction, looting, murder, revenge, and betrayal of a large social segment of the Iraqi Shiites after they came to power after 2003, as they did not build their country in which they grew up and lived in the embrace of its society knowing what wars and the totalitarian regime did for it from poverty, displacement and squandering of Iraq's money. Professor Dakhil Hassan Jarryu (former president of Basra University and former president of the University of Science and Technology during the rule of Saddam Hussein, who is from the Shiite community and from the South) answers this major social problem in his article tagged (Weak participation of Shiites in pre-2003 Iraqi governments?) in Al-Hiwar Al-Mutemedin periodic dated 12ᵗʰ July 2020, as he attributed it to the various reasons all of which are limited mainly to the standards and values of the Shiite community, which are the following:

1. The children of the central and southern governorates refrain from enrolling in government schools for a long time, claiming that they teach students science in violation of Islamic law so that they do not deviate from the authority of clerics and thus deprived them

of modern education opportunities, thus delaying their governorate from the rest of the governorates of Iraq and depriving them of government jobs, not to mention leadership positions in which.

2. Their lack of qualifications has limited them from participating in government jobs at various levels for a long period of time at the instigation of some clerics under the false pretext of the rulers' corruption and usurpation of public money in contravention of Islamic law. Hence it is not permitted for employees to receive any salaries from them.

3. The reluctance of most of the Shiites people of the centre and the south of Iraq to join the ranks of the various armed forces.

4. Departing from the trade in which they excelled so much.

5. Not expressing their desire to take over the leadership of Iraq.

It has become clear, then, what the tails of the Iranian government from Shiites of Iraq have done in terms of sabotage, killing, looting and corruption in government institutions and their inability to rebuild, develop or development throughout their rule of more than seventeen years is due to the lack of scientific, medical, engineering, and administrative skills and competencies that enable them to lead the country in another sense. Neither the Sunnis nor the Christians had any party to the lack of these skills and competencies among the Shiites, but rather the clerics of their sect prevented them from doing so. And what they did after 2003 is the result of what they were brought up on in their sect by not being educated and acquiring technical, professional, and scientific skills that prevented them from actively and mentally participating in governance because of their backward and metaphysical thinking. All that was done on purpose to guarantee the obeying of their sectarian authority. In other words, they have been taught false teachings that harmed them and made them be passive and irresponsible in building the homeland and refrain from serving the people. This is a catastrophe caused by the clerics of the Shiite community, so they became insane on their followers and reflected on Iraqi society in the twenty-first century. They gave a clear picture of their inefficiency and skill in science, knowledge, construction, development, and reform, but they excelled in plundering, theft, sabotage, and treason for foreigners. At the same time, they plunged them into doctrinal fallacies that were filled with myths, narratives and stories that led to the primacy of imaginary perceptions over the historical mind in order to generate a specific faith that is inseparable from the imaginative social thoughts. They made the piousness as doctrine (in the act of hiding the real belief), the sanctification of shrines, for them, taking them as (holy) shrines, Circum-walking and making

88

pilgrimages to them. In fact, most of their beliefs stem from ancient Persian, such as the sanctification of homes and personalities, insulting the Companions and consider them infidels. In Ashura, during which the Shiites proceed to flog themselves and wound their children so that blood spills from them and stains their skin as an expression of sadness and remorse over the killing of Hussein (may God be pleased with him) in Karbala. Therefore, ignorance and lack of education of the Shiite sect is mainly due to the men of their sect in order to make them subject to and obey their religious authority by flooding them with the following:-

1.   Preventing them from acquiring modern science and knowledge.

2.   Being immersed in historical events that cannot be fixed.

3.   Notify them of sadness and remorse for the killing of Hussein (may God be pleased with him).

4.   Not to use the rational interpretation, but rather the narrative.

5.   Stimulating the spirit of self-flagellation and exaggerating the manifestations of sadness and crying over the ruins.

The spur of the problem, therefore, lies in the teachings of the Shiite clerics who have gone crazy over their sect and Iraqi society and offended the reputation and history of modern Iraq. This is the historical analytical logic behind what the tails of Iran have achieved in Iraq who donated revenge against Iraqis and Iraq on behalf of the Magi Persians. Everything that has happened in Iraq after 2003 is the result of what the Shiite sect men planted in the members of their sect, and they bear the following:-

1.   They Insulted the Ja`fari creed in distorting its teachings in order to serve their domination and their sectarian influence.

2.   Deprivation of the sect's members from education and work in leading official institutions.

3.   Preventing them from serving governmental and military institutions.

It is therefore clear that they have committed crimes against their sect and the Iraqi society and disbelieved in the right of religion, and are hostile to the Qur'an and the Creator. This fact leads to that the clerics (wearers of the turbans) have deprived the members of their sect of free-thinking, used religion to serve them by keeping their followers follow them blindly and convert them to rabble, absurd and bohemians, like a herd of sheep.

Turning to the theoretical framing of this problematic phenomenon, it can be said that the clerics nourished the sensations, feelings, and affection of these followers instead of feeding their rational thinking, whether it was in their relations from the historical events of the caliphate selection after the death of Prophet Mohammed (PUH), or in the killing of Hussein (God pleased on him). They used these feelings to prove their presence in the social structure through the teachings that they gained from the leaders of their sect, and hence their existential interests became linked to their feelings rather than to their rational thinking. This state of affairs continued for several centuries and remained conservative and traditional as a closed heritage without change. In other words, there is a religious authority that leads its followers through its preaching upbringing, inducing them by submitting to feelings and sentiments instead of rational thinking. The purpose of this is to keep them under their authority by dominating their feelings in the name of religion rather than inviting them to be free from its restrictions. This theoretical framing is derived from the theory of the ancient Italian sociologist (Felfredo Pareto 1848-1923), that considers the behaviour, interaction, and social relations of the individual do not originate from the influences of his mind and thinking because he is irrational in his social behaviour, but through his sensations, feelings and affections that directly affect his behaviour, interaction, and social relationships, which in effect are not subject to the authority of the mind and its controls, but rather to the values of its social culture. This situation is repeatedly occurring, and the spread of its dimensions in the society and its relationship with other social phenomena will need to be coordinated so that a schematic drawing can be constructed in order to reach the abstract formulation of social law. This means that it is not ideal in the value of rationality within its behavioural standards. [Al Omer. 1990. p. 28 from the book The Fission of the Social Term].

It is noticeable that the rule of the tails of Iran and the parasites are much crueller than the totalitarian rule. The latter did not take revenge on the Iraqis, did not retaliate from them, did not steal their wealth, but rather preserved their security, developed the best education and medical systems, construct the roads and bridges and power plants, and has a respectable international status among nations and respected the sanctities of his people. Likewise, the number of controlling forces in the rule of the tails is more numerous and stricter (the deep state, militias, economic committees, clerics, religious authorities, and others). It seems it is the fate of Iraqis to be ruled for thirty years by strict authoritarianism (totalitarian) and for more than seventeen years by the tails of Iran (sectarian). The question that imposes its self here is why all of this is happening to the Iraqis? Is it because they are solid (out of toughness) and holders of opinion, awareness, and argumentation to be subjugated by more than one foreign power? If the Iranians were colonizing Iraq directly and not through their tails, they would not have done the same as their avenging tails did? Rather, less and they would steal less than their tails who plundered for themselves and their Iranian masters. The tails have been spreading bribery, forgery, and embezzlement among all state employees without shame or shyness. They practised it openly, which was not prevalent in the past, before the American occupation only slightly, while now it has become an accepted phenomenon and part of the official deal. This is due to the fact that senior Iraqi officials, from the prime minister through to ministers, passing through religious, political parties, armed militias, general managers, governors, and even the police and the military are all looking for bribes. They take an imitation of their higher officials, and here the theory (Gabriel Tard, an ancient French sociologist) applies in modelling, simulation and imitation that comes from the bottom up or from the lower class to the upper and not vice versa. But despite all of this, the Iranians despise the Iraqis (and especially their tails), whether they are Arab Shiites, Persians, Sunnis, Kurds, or Turkmen. Even when Iraqi officials go to Tehran on official missions and delegations, they are not received with respect, official processions and the raising of the Iraqi flag. Rather, they deal with them as the master's treatment of the slave or feudal lord with the peasant who cultivates and takes care of his land. It means that Iraqi officials feel inferior, politically and ethnically, in front of their masters, who do not have any respect and appreciation for them, so they are humiliated and submissive when they meet with the rulers of Iran. They behave like rabbits in front of the Iranians, lions in front of the Iraqis, and foxes among them. Was it not for the presence of the Iranian tails in Iraq, Iran would not have been able to dominate Iraq and the Iraqis? The Iranians tried for a period of eight years in a fierce war, but they were not able except now and only with the presence of their tails, who provided the Iranian regime with all means to systematically penetrate into the Iraqi body, rip its guts and suck its blood. They expressed their hatred and grudge for the Iraqis, Arabs, and Islam without thanking their tails for the financial, military, and political services they have provided to them. Rather, they despise them and deal with them in their country with all arrogance, contempt, and disrespect while still, the tails are submissive to them. Such a submissive mentality is in exchange for the Iranian support to them in power because the tails know that the Iraqis do not want them, and they have been rejected by the Iraqi society as they are parasitic components and failed to represent Iraq rightly. They do not have any respect, importance, ideology and have no role other than representing the Persians. It remains to be noted in this context; how were they able to rule a society of diverse ethnicities and religions while they did not possess a collective base nor the political and administrative experience? They have lived as parasites outside Iraq, ignorant of urbanization, progression, and development, pedantic to religious fraud against idiots, rabble, and simples? The answer is that they did not come, but rather they were installed by the invading and colonial American government after it fought a devastating war of all kinds to take over Iraq. Because most of them fought with them against Iraq during Saddam's rule. Now that more than a decade has passed since their inauguration, will they continue in their positions? The answer is no because they represent an ill anomaly in the sphere of governance of a society that does not know permanent submissiveness or continuous servitude. The youth Shiite sect in the south and centre of Iraq rejected them because they took advantage of the sect and relied on the Iranian support to rule Iraq. The Sunni youth, however, in the western region preceded them for several years when they rose up and revolted peacefully against them in the years 2011 and 2019. In these uprisings, the youth called them thieves in the name of religion and called Iran to exit Iraq because their tails were failures and stigmatized both from their sect and the Sunni community, but they remained clinging to the rule because they knew their future fate, so they used firepower and coercive police with stubbornness in front of the local and international media agencies.

Finally, it can be said that the Shiite youth has freed itself from the domination of the Shiite sect, demanding their contribution to nation-building, political and social change, and national identity. They also liberated themselves from the neglect of the parasitic ruling class in the name of

95

religion and demanded its removal and expulsion from the government. This is very promising and the first drops of collective awareness, which are the harbinger of goodness in the rise of an Iraqi generation that rejects religious sectarianism, foreign domination, revenge against Iraqis and the plunder of their wealth. Before leaving this topic, few questions need to be asked:-

1. If these tails are really the rulers of a country, then why are they stealing their country's money?

2. If these tails are really the rulers of a country, why do they spoil the institutions of their country?

3. If these tails are really the rulers of a country, why would they dismantle their country's factories and sell them?

4. If these tails are really the rulers of a country, why do they smuggle their country's energy resources abroad?

5. If these tails are really the rulers of a country, why do they get bribed from merchants and investors?

6. If these tails were really the rulers of a country, why did they not build schools and hospitals for their countrymen?

7. If these tails are really the rulers of a country, why do they smuggle their money abroad?

8. If these tails are really the rulers of a country, why do they rely on the sectarian authority and not the collective base in their decisions?

9. If these tails are really the mates' rulers of a country, why do they have armed militias and have not relied on military and security institutions?

10. If these tails are really the rulers of a country, why do they spoil the judiciary of their country?

11. If these tails were really the rulers of a country, why did they expel millions of Iraqis from their cities?

12. If these tails were really the rulers of a country, why did they allow ISIS to occupy Mosul?

13. Why did these tails not leave Iraq when they knew the Sunni, Shiite and Kurdish components did not support them?

14. Why did these tails not leave power when the Shiite masses came out against their rule?

15. Why were these tails not ashamed when they were branded as thieves and agents for foreigners by the people?

16. Why were these tails not ashamed of the contempt of the American and Iranian governments for them when meeting with them? Is it not enough for them to understand their true image in the eyes of others, that they are villains, traitors, disgrace, and agents that neither their masters nor their countrymen

respect? Indeed, the theory (Charles Harton Cooley, a sociologist at the University of Chicago) about a person in the mirror says that a person sees his social image through the judgments of others around him. So, this theory does not apply to them because they are not normal humans. Even criminals know their image through the judgments of the police, the judiciary and other criminal groups. However, these tails did not understand and did not pay attention to the judgment of others over them, including the Iraqis and the Iranian and American governments. They are, then, professionally corrupt criminals, who have fallen away from social controls, decomposed from them, and are stripped of their national identity. Is it not enough for us to say about them that they are neither Iraqis nor representatives of the Iraqi people? They are representatives of the occupier and the Iranian government which are revenging from the Iraqis and greedy for Iraq's wealth. They have profaned the history of Iraq. Let us explain in detail a theory (Cooley, 1864-1929) about the reality of the traitors' parties that ruled Iraq on behalf of the Iranian regime. The theory says: "For others to judge the individual and provide him with their observations and directions, in particular the judgment of those close to him and those who are concerned, he has a great and effective impact in shaping his behaviour and thinking because he interacts with them and finds his image in their opinions, evaluation and criticism of him, and when this happens his belonging to them crystallizes and commit to their says, thoughts and desires which he can then take and consider as lead by example" [Al Omer. 1982. p. 201]. In other words, Cooley said: "The human self looks at itself through the judgment of others around it who are important and are concerned with how it appears in their view when they judge it. The human self, therefore, acts in the light of their judgment and evaluation as if they are the mirror of the society where the soul characteristics can be seen through its image reflection on this mirror" [Al Omer. 1982. p.202]. When using this theory to interpret the behaviour of the ruling traitor parties in Iraq, it can be said that members of the ruling parties have been condemned and stigmatized by Iraqi society as thieves, murderers, corrupt, and agents of Iran and America in the demonstrations of two million Shiites, Sunnis, and Kurds in southern, central, western, and northern Iraq. The denotators chanted slogans (In the name of religion, the thieves robbed us) and (Get Iran out, Baghdad stays free). For the first time, these parties have felt their end is becoming close, so they mobilised their armed militias to kill, imprison, and torture the demonstrators as if they were enemies, not the people of their society. It means that they did not respect the people's judgment over them and did not stop stealing the wealth of Iraq and corrupting its institutions but rather increased their loyalty to the rulers of Iran to prove their servitude and enslavement in exchange for their support in ruling Iraq while they continued to steal Iraqi wealth and handed it over to the Iranian regime which its economy started to collapse under the economic sanction. Not only that, but they carried out all the Iranian orders to kill and assassinate the Iraqi scholars, pilots and military leaders who fought Iran before 2003. That is besides stealing Iraq's treasuries, destroying its economy and industry, disrupting its movement's march, spreading terrorism and sectarian strife, and establishing armed militias for them not to defend them, but to kill everyone who does not submit to them or everyone who does not walk in their march. These parties are Iranian tails riding and driving them as mules. The significance of my words is that these parties have coincided with the orders and decisions of the rulers of Iran because they are their backers and protectors during their refuge with him and not their belief in the mandate of the jurist or the Ja'fari school because they do not possess the belief, religious philosophy, or Iraqi national identity. They are the dastardliest, homeless people who are shunned from their local community. They have not been respected and considered by others, so they did not identify and harmonise with the Iraqi masses who pronounced their judgment and condemnation because they are agents (tails) of Iran and stole Iraq wealth and gave it to them and took revenge on the Iraqis, killing, imprisonment and deportation. They did not feel shame or inferiority when millions of Iraqi Shiites, Sunnis and Kurds came out, calling them traitors, thieves, and agents. I wanted here to reach the (Cooley) theory that was applied to the agents' parties in their solidarity and identification with the rulers of Iran. This is my proof of their distinguished role as agents and their outright betrayal. They have nothing to do with the Iraqis and Iraq, but their association is with Iran is confirmed and evident. In this respect, the rules and directives of the Iranian regime on them are especially important and cannot be departed from because the traitors of Iraq are Iran creation. Therefore, these parties contaminated the reputation of Iraq, tarnished its image in front of the world, committed crimes against its citizens, smuggled its wealth and precious treasures, and spread corruption in it. In short, it can be said that (Cooley's) theory has clarified the treason of the ruling parties in Iraq and confirmed their nonbelonging and their lack of patriotic feeling through their indifference to stigmatizing the masses with the worst and ugliest disgrace stigmas. They, therefore, killed and imprisoned all of those who do not accept them. The loyalty of these agents and their puppet parties to the Iranian regime is mechanical loyalty (according to the description of Emile Durkheim, a French sociologist); that is, they move in a complete movement with all its parts and staff without hesitation when they receive the orders from Iranian. this is because their relationship is reciprocal relation in exchange to support as per the contemporary American sociologist (George Homens), which means that the Iranian regime provides political supports to the traitors' rule and their armed militias in exchange for carrying out his orders to take revenge on the Iraqi people and the plunder of Iraq wealth to save Iran's collapsing economy. It is clear that the existence of these parties, which were recruited by Iran, depends on the presence of the Iranian regime in power, and they will disappear, and their members and their militias will run away from Iraq (diaspora) once the Iranian regime collapses. They neither have a mass base in Iraq nor sectarian loyalty to their sect. They return, carrying their shame and disgrace with them after the Shiites of Iraq disowns them. Moreover, they will be chased by the International Police (Interpol) to arrest them and return the stolen money from Iraq. This is the definite end of every criminal, saboteur, and outlaw. The other fact about these parties is that they have turned the naturally balanced equation into two conflicting and contradictory poles. As it is known, the parties, as official organizations in advanced urban and industrial societies, are mediators between the society and the government. They defend the rights of the marginalized, the deported, the unemployed, the poor, the illiterate, the slums, respect the opinion of the other, and apply justice between segments of society. However, the traitors of the puppet parties in Iraq after 2003 projected themselves as agents of a foreign government hostile to Iraq (the Iranian clerics' government), which used them as striking forces to revenge on the Iraqis on its behalf because it had historical revenge and ambitions to confiscate Iraqi wealth. In return for supporting these parties to stay in the rule of Iraq, they exchanged benefits and interests with the

Iranian regime, while they worked in disgraceful style to implement everything that the Iranians requested from them, such as destroying the economy of Iraq, widening the gap between the classes of society, destroying the education and medical systems, not opening job opportunities for young people, and igniting the fire of sedition between Shiites and Sunnis and inciting the Kurds are against the Arabs, dividing Iraq into warring regions. They punished everyone demanding his legitimate rights, using violence, practising bloody terrorism, isolating residential areas and neighbourhoods with concrete barriers, destroying everything that is useful for the economy, flooding the markets with expired Iranian goods, and harnessing Iraqi funds to compensate the deficit in the Iranian economy at the expense of the Iraqi economy, fighting Arab nationalism, distorting religious teachings, and getting the rabble and the poor occupied by practising religious rituals that are not required by the Ja'fari sect. In conclusion, these parties represent an anomaly state in the official organizations in the twenty-first century. They have drowned the Iraqi society with economic, social, and psychological problems, which are the antithesis of the spirit of the age. They are hostile to the people and usurp their rights in favour of the hostile foreigner who wants to revenge on the Iraqis. It is a disaster and scandal of the times, as such parties are supposed to demanding justice and defending the marginalized, the poor and the unemployed.

Finally, we come to define the characteristics of these parties:

i. They do not represent the official organizations mediating between the people and the government in the interest of serving the people.

ii. They represent the Iranian government in Iraq par excellence against the Iraqis.

iii. They failed to be in harmony with the Iraqi society. Rather, they are identical to the Iranian regime.

iv. They have armed militias that are used against Iraqis.

v. They recruited their members from the Shiite community.

vi. They tampered with and then humiliated the Iraqis, leaving them in an insecure and unsafe state.

vii. They are not political parties, but rather criminal groups and gangs with specific specializations, which are:

    a. A group specialized in white-collar crimes (in institutions and ministries that engage in theft, smuggling, forgery and abuse of influence).

b. A group specialized in crimes of white and black turbans, which are the placement of non-standardised values in place of normal standardised in the value system.

c. A group specialized in murder, rape, bank robbery, the proceeds of border and customs outlets, and oil smuggling through partisan militias.

The Sunni Parties Are Secondary Tails to the Main Tails of the Iranian Regime in Iraq

The Sunni component is not far from the Shiite scene. It is in conflict with itself for the sake of opportunistic interests and spoils. The Sunni parties suffer from leadership struggles (implicit struggles) in order to reap the benefits of those who will be a leader in the upcoming Sunni arena. These leaderships were characterized by leadership narcissism and arrogance, relying on money and the media in the service of political influence, with a loss of principle in action, a severe fluctuation in positions, and inflecting failing the allies to satisfy new allies that reached the point of opportunism. In the sense that they are not official political or social organizations with a doctrine, controls, and an honourable history in public work and mediating between Sunnis and the government or Iraqis and the leadership, but rather a gathering of individuals who met in private interests who used the sectarian (Sunni) cover to give themselves a sectarian characteristic that entices the mob and the demons in the Sunni regions for the sake of Winning them as votes not to serve their needs and develop their regions. Note that Iraq has lived under a secular rule for more than thirty years under the rule of the Baath Party, and it does not differentiate between Shiites and Sunnis. But some of the bankrupt people in the masses used the heresy of the Sunni community in order to use it only as their human repository. This is a pernicious distinction that tears apart the Iraqi social fabric and creates religious discrimination between Muslims that later led to bloody conflicts between the two sects exploited by bankrupt elements of the people who want to ascend the authoritarian peace through them, not out of love for religion or Iraq and Iraqis, but rather to achieve sick interests at the expense of the public interest. These Sunni parties are:-

1.   The Iraqi Islamic Party led by Dr. Mohsen Abdel-Hamid.

2.   The Association of Muslim Scholars led by Dr. Harith Al-Dhari.

3.   The Islamic Party led by Salim Al-Jubouri.

4.   Motahidoon Coalition led by Osama Al-Nujaifi.

5.   Al-Arabiya coalition led by Saleh Al-Mutlaq.

6.   Movement (Al hel) led by Khamis Al-Khanjar. Then there are Al-Halbousi, Karbouli, and Abu Mazen, representing the Sunnis.

There is no harm in asking about these factional blocs to the effect that if they all aim to serve the Sunni community, why were they not in the form of one organization (one party) that brings together all of these? Doesn't it mean that each group has a personal interest that is far from the public interest? If they really are Sunnis, do they have a religious and militant background in the service of Iraqis? And if they

108

are politicians, why are they using the sectarian cover for them? Is it to increase their belonging? These groups spurred the distinction between the Sunnis, the components of Iraqi society, and the Shiites. They are divided groups, not united, hypocritical, not sincere, that serve their founders, not Iraq and the Iraqis. As for the armed Sunni militias, they are:

1. The base of jihad in Mesopotamia.

2. ISIS of Iraq.

3. Ansar Al-Sunna Army.

4. Ansar Al-Islam Army.

5. Al Mujahideen Army.

6. The Islamic Army in Iraq.

7. Al Jihadi Resistance Army.

8. Muhammad's Army.

9. Al Ishreen Revolution Brigades.

10. The Islamic Front for the Iraqi Resistance.

In order to demonstrate what I was mentioned above, the reasons for the failure of these parties in their national, religious, and political claims are recorded:

1. It rejected the new changed political reality altogether (that is, after 2003 when America invaded and occupied Iraq and toppled Saddam's regime) and stood firmly against it in a desperate attempt to turn the clock back.

2. It showed violent enmity against the Kurds and the Kurdish parties, especially the Islamic party

affiliated with the Muslim Brotherhood-led by the Vice President of the Republic accused of terrorism, Tariq Al-Hashemi.

3. The withdrawal of the Sunni Iraqiya List from the parliament hall in protest against the election of Jalal Talabani as president of Iraq in 2010 because he was from the Kurdish component.

4. The blind racial hatred that the Sunni Arabs displayed towards the Kurds and their efforts to undermine their legitimate national gains prompted the Kurds to support the Shiite parties in taking power.

5. Boycott the parliamentary elections.

6. Their intra (with the Kurdish and Shiite parties) and implicit struggles (within the one Sunni party) for the acquisition of ministries.

7. Their alliance with the Shiite parties at the elections in order to obtain special privileges and interests that resulted in the destruction of the Sunni governorates and their backwardness in terms of services and the presence of thousands of absentees in prisons in addition to the millions of refugees in the camps, including the displaced and the unemployed, such as Al-Halbousi and Khamis Al-Khanjar who fought over the ministries. And it even reached the higher positions such even the Sunni clerics and the

president of the Al-Imam Al Adham University wrestled over private interests and their seizure of mosques such as Umm Al-Tabbool Mosque and the declaration of Sheikh Mahdi Al-Sumaida'i himself as the Mufti of the Sunnis, relying on his relationship with the Shiite parties and Iran, so they called themselves the Sunnah of Conquest and the Sunnah of Reform.

8. The purchase of ministerial positions where the post of Minister of Electricity reached $5.0 million and of Defence $20.0 million.

9. The Sunnis have their clear thieves, and they have their way of emptying the state treasury through banquets, gifts, and the media, in order to promote and polish the image of the Sunni Endowment and its head Abd Al-Latif Hamim.

10. Hundreds of documents leaked from the Sunni Endowment Bureau, which showed huge numbers wasted from the endowment budget over the years of 2016, in which the head of the court spent 220 million dinars on gifts, including those gifts, the original Rolex watches.

11. One of the ways of corruption in the Sunni endowment is allocating large sums for the restoration of mosques that do not exist. In 2015, the endowment spent ID14.8 billion from its budget for

the restoration of fake mosques not listed in the state records. Similarly, a huge amount of money was spent to restore the headquarter building of the Sunni Endowment while it has no building. The Endowment was not aware of the disbursement of that amount, as the Umm Al-Qura Mosque in Baghdad was one of the most frequent sites of the Sunni endowment that was used to steal the endowment budget. In 2015, the Sunni Endowment contracted with a number of newspapers, websites, and satellite channels for a total amount of ID4.0 billion in order to promote the activities of the endowment and its president, and one of those channels was the Al-Hadath channel, which is owned by Al-Humim, the son of the President of the Endowment. As for the Iraqi Fiqh Society of the Endowment itself, ID2.0 billion were embezzled, and only ID0.9 billion million were spent from it (it is one of the white turbans crimes).

12. Jamal Al-Karbouli rigged the elections and bought ministerial posts, in addition to smear and extortion campaigns against his opponents from among the leaders and Sunni political parties, as he embezzled $150 million from the funds of the Red Crescent Organization and was sentenced to 15 years imprisonment and wanted by the International Police

(Interpol). He also stole the donations of the Red Crescent Society and seized donated medicines by the Saudi Red Crescent is estimated at 50 million dollars. The Karbouli family is also accused of dismantling and selling some of the large giant factories of the Ministry of Industry and Minerals, including the copper wire factory in Fallujah, Anbar, Wasit and Babel (it is a white-collar crime). Then Jamal Al-Karbouli owned hotels and cabarets in Belarus to run prostitution through which he invited officials and MPs and filmed them in a show of disgrace with prostitutes, which he used after to blackmail them. He is close to Al Maliki, Saudi Arabia, UAE, and Iran's allies in Iraq.

13. The Sunni parties received financial support from Tehran and moral influences by the Iranian General Qassem Soleimani in order to pressure the Shiite parties and obtain approval for the annexation of some of the Sunni forces that lost the majority of their masses as a result of the flight of party leaders and political figures from their cities occupied by ISIS. This means that the Sunni parties, after the occupation, did not look at the situation of occupied Iraq with a realistic view but rather with an unrealistic one. They made several strategic mistakes that created enemies for them. They are not supposed

113

to have enemies while they are under foreign occupation. But when the Shiite parties seized power and formed armed militias, the Sunni parties were subjected to extortion, falling into financial corruption, and buying ministries, as the Shiite parties did in oil smuggling.

The Sunni clerics, however, were not committed to the teachings of the Islamic religion in: -

i.   Honesty in responsibility and respect for other opinion.

ii.   Racial intolerance against the Kurds, who are Muslims and Iraqis.

iii. Fabricated hostilities with the Shiite community which is Muslim and Iraqi.

iv.   Truthfulness in charters and relationships and non-betrayal.

v.   Theft of public funds which are assigned intended for the saving of the members of their community from asylum, displacement, and absenteeism.

There is no crime in saying: for a patriot who wants to fight and expel the occupier from his homeland, he must first unite its ranks and its social, political, religious, and ethnic components instead of creating conflicts with them because the enemy is one and common to everyone. This is foolish and stupid behaviour that does not come from a patriot, a professional politician or a sane adult person, but from a greedy narcissist who does not know the Iraqi society or religious teaching and has not read the history of Iraq or Islamic history. It is clear that they are driven by the motive of seizing power on their own without getting the Kurds, Shiites, Turkmen, and Christians involved in it. Knowing that some of them hold higher university degrees, unlike the Shiite component during the second and third decade of the last century, as the Sunni clerics had no effect and could not prevent the Sunnis from education and employment in state departments as the Shiite clerics did with their sect members at the time. Having said that, they were still far from their patriotism while concentrating their concern and their efforts on their personal interests to reap the benefits. They, therefore, fell into intra and implicit conflicts, and they used immoral methods to blackmail some politicians, partisans, and parliamentarians. They do not differ from the Shiite players in the political field. Both are using all kinds of corruption for money and higher positions, and the use of the sect, its rabble, and its savvy to support them in parliamentary elections without providing any services in infrastructure, education, health, social care and social security. So far, both of them are the same in theft and abuse of influence and lack of community development and progress, but rather it is dismantling, tearing up, swallowing its rights, and starving its people. In order to scrutinize the above, we ask the following questions: Is loose money, false influence, false power, corruption of the judiciary, the absence of law, and the impersonation of the religious teaching of the sect as a front for financial and political gain that made the formation of self-interest blocs instead of serving the society and the country? Or there are fraudulent people who do not have popular, religious or political bases, supported by foreign powers (Iran, America, Saudi Arabia, Qatar and the Emirates) managed in the shade of the stormy and wavy turmoil after the fall of the political system in 2003 with persecuted feelings among the poor during the previous rule and the immigration of the educated and middle class outside Iraq have made the assertions of groups of opportunists, outreaches, and those who have lost their national identity and religious belief, the right to use the religious sect as a strong shield to protect their falsehood and allegations in order to seize positions and loose wealth? The impersonators of the Sunni sect do not differ from the impersonators of the Shiite sect in terms of their assaults on money and power and their strength gaining from foreigners. The Sunni parties were tails of the Iranian rule in Iraq, as they were used by the Iranians who blackmailed them into being under their leadership and orders. It can be said that both are tails for foreigners and money thieves, and they do not serve Iraq, the Shiites, or the Sunnis but are hostile to both. Therefore, both the Sunni and the Shiite impersonators fell into the swamp of vice. They did not serve but stole

116

Iraq's money and smuggled it abroad. Even the Sunni clerics in the Sunni Endowment were fraudsters and thieves in the name of religion. They took advantage of these legal vacuums, weakening customary controls, distorting religious teachings, converting them from forbidden to permitted, and racing for the powerful influence open to the powerful and wealthy owners, and those have experience in fraud, forgery and embezzlement, with the political support and militia protection in light of the weakness of government security agencies or the absence of their influence or participation with them. This anomalous and unfamiliar phenomenon occurred to the Iraqis by constant intimidation and luring some of them with money while they were unemployed and out of wars that exhausted their powers, which made them join in parties that they know are sectarian to become military elements in their militias to kill, assassinate and rob banks, dismantle factories, and sell them by parties' officials of both sects. It means they practised official criminality with the state's knowledge without being held accountable. It is cancerous chaos that kills all the cells of society, but the authentic society like the Iraqi society cannot live with these cancers because it has an immune system within it represented by the conscious youth, whether they are Shiites or Sunnis who raised their voices several times in 2011, 2015 and 2019, but it was met with police response and fire because they expressed their demands in a civilized manner. These youth will continue their immunity to these cancers and remove them from the Iraqi body. Our place in this discussion is to examine what has been mentioned above to say that the Iraqi society before 2003 is characterized as a social intermixture between its social and sectarian groups that prevailed its cities, neighbourhoods, official institutions, schools, colleges, and family. These are criteria and simulations that sociologists use to define the concept of fanaticism to a category in a multi-ethnic and multi-religious society. However, if the society has a separated white neighbourhood from black neighbourhoods and the white man does not marry the black woman, and there are cities especially for black and other for white like the American society, such a society is described as a society of fanatic to ethnics. Such a situation, in fact, did not exist in Iraqi society before 2003. All state departments are a mixture of Sunnis, Shiites, Kurds, Turkmen, Christians and Muslims without discrimination or allocation. Family wise there are marriages of Sunnis' men from Shiites' women and vice versa without any restriction by the family or the sectarian, and there are neighbourhoods in the cities inhabited by a mixture of Shiites, Sunnis and Kurds And Muslims and Christians without breaks between them. However, the political parties were the ones who created this sedition. Because they did not possess a collective base and roots in the Iraqi society due to their recent formation, they followed

118

this dirty path to gain voices quickly and massively in the parliamentary elections through the sectarian line-up. They have no ideology or national affiliation; hence they were empowered by the foreigner and caused this sedition so that they appear on the political stage and obtaining high positions. With such a selfish action, these parties have transformed the Iraqi society from a social Intermixture into three Heterogenous components society. Because of their stupidity, narrow thinking, and the shallowness of their social and political knowledge, they did not realise that the empowering by foreigners will not be for free or without return. It requires submissiveness and making concessions to the empowering power, which are the sacrificing of Iraqi resources rather than the love of that power. The fabrication of sectarian strife has torn apart the social fabric and divided the city neighbourhoods into sectarian residential areas. This crime has been committed by the members of parties, which are supposed to be the intermediary organizations between the people and the government to mediate and achieve the people demands and transferring their complaints to the decision-makers in order to help them in their livelihood. They did the opposite and instead exploited the people and made them human warehouses and fuel for their political fires. They use the people in elections, stealing money allocated to immigrants and refugees, vandalizing their mosques, tampering with their money, and spreading moral

119

corruption among their ranks by selling drugs, opening places for gambling, trafficking in smuggling money and individuals. They have opened Iraq and converted it to be a hotbed for international gangs and mafias in money laundering, arms dealings, smuggling cultural relics and secret official documents, and others. Therefore, there is no difference in the crimes of the Sunnis and the Shiites Parties. They have the same objectives in fabricating sectarianism, empowering their parties by the foreigner, and bringing him to Iraq to control the trade, politics, and fate of Iraq. They assumed the sect's name to defraud the commoners of both sects and allowing the Iranian government to take revenge on Iraqi scholars, military leaders, and youth activists. Moreover, they fabricated civil war and practising white-collar crimes in government institutions and crimes with white and black turbans in mosques, Husseiniyas and religious shrines.

The State Crimes:

On top of the above-mentioned crimes, there are the State crimes that are committed by the government as follows:-

1.   Isolating some areas, restricting transportation, and delimiting it between the different regions.

2.   Inequality between the sects of society.

3.   Waste of energy sources.

4.   Indifference to the suffering of Iraqis.

5. Annoying qualified and experienced staff and denying them from appointment in higher degrees in state institutions.

6. Funding immoral interests.

7. Financing anti-social armed militias.

8. Squandering the wealth of Iraq to polish religious symbols.

9. Presenting bribery of government employees in order to obtain work contracts.

10. Feeding and encouraging terrorism.

11. Appointment of employees in government jobs by the sect without any consideration to the laws.

12. Creating fake (illusion) jobs that do not exist at the level of reality.

13. Failure to regulate the insurance of important medical services.

14. Weak measures that are unable to meet official obligations but are imposed on the state governmental mechanisms.

15. Weakness of victims of state crimes to defend their lost rights and the injustice inflicted upon them by the state employees, especially retirees.

16. Random and moody directions and orders that only serve the narcissism of the official.

17. The use of violent methods against the demonstrators.

18.   Negligence and restriction in granting licenses and permits to the general public while facilitating them to the ruling class and its entourage.

19.   Concluding commercial deals with countries that sell them fraudulent, poorly made, or forged goods in their logo and their source of manufacturing origin or selling them spoiled and expired foodstuffs that are not suitable for human use.

20.   The emergence of a voracious commercial and political layer that has no roots in the financial and political soil has made it competes in its greed, thirst, recklessness, and corruption in the exploitation of the public. These crimes are additional to the crimes committed by the Shiite and Sunni parties that have lasted for more than seventeen years.

After this digression about the futility, theft, and corruption of the Sunni parties, I present some detailed studies on the Sunni House since 2003 and its parties in Iraq, namely:

After the fall of the capital, Baghdad, in April 2003, Sunni Islamist, nationalist and liberal political parties participated for the first time in the political process. It developed its political organizations and programs on Western foundations benefiting from Western research houses, despite the contradiction between the public political demands of these parties, movements, and groupings, and the political orientations of the Iraqi regime in the stages (post-2005). The dominant Shiite parties have deliberately exploited their influence in government and pursued central Sunni, Islamic and liberal leaders, using some laws on (terrorism and integrity) (2006-2013), which prohibit the establishment of parties or even the exercise of political action freely and openly from limiting their activities. As happened with Adnan Al-Dulaimi, Muhammad Al-Daini, Rafe Al-Issawi, Jamal Al-Karbouli, Dhafir Al-Ani, Khamis Al-Khanjar, Omar Al-Karbouli, Athil Al-Nujaifi, Ahmad Abdullah Al-Jubouri, Salim Al-Jubouri and Hamdi Hassoun ... Sunni leaders faced the problem of the absence of a symbol or a high reference that could hold the strings of their unity when disagreement/conflict which took place due to the internal strife and the external and internal challenges that faced the Iraqi political system after 2003. That was why Sunni Arab regions and governorates were prompted to support the political movement of these parties in a pessimistic and angry manner without totally rejecting the regional project of the Sunni areas or the complete boycott of the political process. Most of the Sunni political parties received Gulf, regional, and international support, material, moral and political, and this enabled them to manoeuvre with partners who are more organized and have a rhythm officer. They managed to have a partnership of 28 to 30 per cent of government and parliamentary quotas. A share that the

Sunnis in the Governing Council were satisfied with after 2003. It then became a curse associated with their presence in the political system, which empowered their criticism and anger against the ruling political system in several stages, the most prominent of which was the end of 2012, with their retracting mood of coexistence and partnership with Shiite political parties in the height of the Arab Spring. The Iraqi regime needed stability, economic, military, moral and political support to face the challenges of the transition from dictatorship to democracy in addition to regional challenges represented in the Iraqi neighbourhood, especially Iran, Syria and the Gulf, and to face the internal challenges of armed operations against the American occupation, and to enter into a clash with a wide spectrum from the sympathetic Iraqi street. Therefore, the occupation turned a blind eye to the activity of the Shiite and Kurdish parties in exchange for its militancy towards the Sunni parties in general and the left-wing and political parties that support the resistance in particular, in an attempt to avoid the dangers of these challenges. The transition to democracy and political participation came as an attempt by the occupation and the political system in order to involve the Sunni, Shiite and Kurdish parties, other cultures, nationalism and others in decision-making and the transfer of power in a peaceful manner, but on the condition that the new political system participates in its attempts to face internal and external

124

challenges, avoid the risks of threatening the system, and calming Resistant Sunni and Shiite political street as is the case after the events of 2005 and the events of 2008, and up to the stage of protests sit-ins in the Sunni provinces of 2012-2013. The transformation to political pluralism was not a political option, neither for the regime nor for nationalist, liberal and Islamic political parties. Laws, regulations, and legislation restricted the political and partisan activity of the Sunni and Kurdish parties and minorities and did not give the right to these parties to exercise the rotation of power through legislative elections. It was also not a political option for the Sunni and liberal parties through its national, material, and moral association with regional and external parties that do not believe in the control of the Shiite parties, which are in harmony with Iran and political participation. Although the Shiite parties stipulate in their internal regulations on democracy and the rotation of power, they did not adopt democracy in their practical practices inside Its systems, and this was evident in the 2010 elections when it took the premiership from the Sunni alliance by judicial decision and was given to the Shiite alliance, and it did not take the rotation of power or political participation since its inception, despite its calls and demands from the political system for the rotation of power and democracy.

Parties of The Sunni House: The political and partisan participation in 2010 was a victim of mistrust and the difference between the ruling system and the Sunni parties. These parties show hostility and threat to the ruling system, and the ruling system exchanges this policy with them. In defence of each party for its legitimacy and continuity, there were attempts in 2011 to dissolve the government, but the attempt failed. In the 2018 elections, the Sunni parties, despite the political system's support for their role, could not create a unified alliance, as they were divided into Sunni Arab and Sunni liberal, and they lost influence in the transformation of democratic political participation in their activities overtly and covertly with the tribal - crowd and the rising popular areas after the liberation of their cities from ISIS. Therefore, the political Shiism took control of their cities electorally and even at the level of senior executive positions in the provinces. In addition to the above, there are a number of political, financial, legal, and subjective challenges facing Sunni political parties in general and Sunni political alliances calling for the manufacture of a Sunni symbol or reference in particular. The Sunni parties, liberal, nationalist, and Islamic, which were and still criticize the system of government dominated by the Shiite Islamic parties, and are trying to establish an alternative political system, must harness their programs and ideology to contribute to the governance of the Iraqi state and its institutions so that the system reassures the goals of these parties, and they march together towards political participation and the rotation of power. In 2020, Iraqi governments are required to develop and update legislative frameworks and laws governing the activity of political parties that have limited their activities and affected their capabilities and organizational building, especially during the October 2019 protests, in order to participate in political development, support democracy and political participation, and enhance Trust between parties and the state, because the relationship between parties and governments was and still is a relationship that lacks confidence, so each side blames the other, The governments accuse the parties of the inadequacy and weakness of their programs, and their inability to convince the people to join them, while the parties accuse the governments of impeding democracy and political participation, as a result of their disruptive procedures and laws for the parties. Therefore, each party must concede its positions to bring viewpoints closer and restore confidence between them in order to contribute to the creation of real democracy and political participation in the development of democratic life. The current and future stage requires uniting the Sunni parties of all their affiliations within an alliance with a leadership council that has its own political organization and clear rhetoric, and this is possible when Al-Halbousi, Al-Khanjar and Al-Najafi agree on a unified vision that enables the Sunni component to trust them and support them electively and politically under the name of the Sunni national trend. This will enable them to compete with other political formations and gain a new democratic mass base, and competes in political participation, leading to the rotation of power.

The Sunni Jurisprudential Reference: The Baath regime has worked, since the era of President Ahmed Hassan Al-Bakr, to avoid having a legitimate reference for the Sunnis of Iraq. Rather, the Mufti has become forgotten, and he was Marginalized in the Sunni sense. The Mufti at the time of the Baath is a Sufi, and he should be close to the relationships and recommendation of the leader of the Baath Party, Izzat Al-Douri, such as Sheikh Abd Al-Razzaq Al-Saadi and Sheikh Rafe Al-Rifai. Each one of them is surrounded by a group of Saddam's intelligence and security, and they are the ones who tell him in his ear what to do and how to act and perhaps what fatwa he gives! Since 2004, Sheikh Harith Al-Dhari tried to reach the unification of the leadership of the fatwa for the Sunnis of Iraq through his leadership of the (Muslim Scholars Association). But when he departed from the visions of the Muslim Brotherhood and their political speech, most of them rejected him, so he left Iraq and the Sunni parties, and the Sunni Endowment preachers promoted against his political discourse and his defence of the solution by armed resistance in more than one dialogue on Al-Jazeera and others. Though they bet on its success, they know that the image the Baath regime drew for

128

the Mufti of the Sunnis of Iraq may fail the project of mobilising a Sunni majority to follow and rally around a Sunni jurisprudential reference represented by the (Fiqh Council) of senior Iraqi Sunni scholars. As for the Salafists, they had an attempt to create their own Fatwa House at the end of 2003, which was brought by Sheikh Abdul Hamid Al-Rashidi, Dr Mahmoud Al-Mashhadani, Dr Fakhri Al-Qaisi, Sheikh Mahdi Al-Sumaida'i and Sheikh Abdul Sattar Al-Janabi, and they established what is known as (The Supreme Commission for Advocacy, Guidance and Fatwa), but they failed for many reasons, most notably: funding, because they do not have support from the Sunni endowment, and most of the sheikhs are preoccupied with fighting the Americans, and their division on the issue of political work and the position on democracy and the rule of writing the constitution and the rule of entry into parliament and the government! As for Sufis, they relied from the beginning on the traditions established for them by the Baath regime in the presidency of the House of Ifta, known to them as (the Mufti of Iraq), where after the scholar Abdul Karim Al-Mudaris, this title was assumed by his most senior student, Sheikh Jamal Abdul Karim Sl-Daban, who headed the House of Ifta of Sufism until In 2007. After his death, Sheikh Rafai Al-Rifai, famous for his pro-Baathist positions, was chosen as the Izzat Al-Douri wing. As for the Saadi family, they are despite their possession of the repertoire of knowledge and

129

advancement in it, but they were known for their support for the Sunni Arab depth and their pursuit of isolating the traditional jurisprudential influence from political action. As for Sheikh Dr Ahmad Al-Kubaisi, he has the courage to criticize the Companions, and his tongue praises the Shiites more than the Sunnis. Therefore, he lost his acceptance of the common people of Iraq. Moreover, his intellectual transformations throughout his history between the thought of the Tahrir group and the thought of the Brotherhood and the Sufi at times and political Shiism at other times eroded his credibility.

Sunni Political Dualism: The arrival of the young liberal politician, Muhammad Al-Halbousi, to the presidency of Parliament is a useful and fruitful experience for the liberal youth group that was disturbed by the monopoly of the Sunni Islamist parties that are exclusively allied with them. Such presidency moved between Mahmoud Al-Mashhadani, the Salafi Islamist, and Iyad Al-Samarrai, from the Islamic party, then Osama Al-Nujaifi, the nationalist conservative allied with the Islamists, then Salim Al-Jubouri, on the Islamic party. It is assumed that the leaders of the Islamic trends, as well as the nationalist and liberal trends, review this sudden rise that occurred at a time of the decline of the Sunni Islamic political trend in order to draw lessons to help them in their future political work. Al-Halbousi bloc also belongs to the classification of liberal

Sunni parties with a nationalist depth that rife with splits, in addition to the growing competition with a former ally, Sheikh Khamis Al-Khanjar, who is considered as one of the most important parties that removed the Sunni Islamist parties from the participation in the leadership of the Sunni political house and monopolizing the most important positions of Sunni representation according to the custom of quotas. Then, the 2018 elections brought a new bilateral setup, a major and a secondary one, to lead the Sunni political house, liberal Al-Halbousi and the nationalist Al-Khanjar. Al-Halbousi bilateral represented of Ahmed Abdullah Abu Mazen and Falah Zaidan Al-Lahibi, with a total of 61 parliamentarians, and with Al-Khanjar bilateral represented by of Al-Najafi and Muthanna Al-Samarrai with a total of 14 parliamentarians. The experience that president Al-Halbousi relies on, with his bilateral in dealing with the liberal political presence, is a catalyst in containing other Sunni parties with tribal, leftist, and religious stripes and improving the Sunni regional climate to support stability and reconstruction through a fruitful calm with Shiite forces close to Iran, and open interaction with American interests and their allies in the Arab depth. Sheikh Al-Khanjar's problem, along with his bilateral, revolved around the integration of the relationship between the Sunnis (as an Arab nationalism in Iraq) and the Sunnah (as a juristic community imitating the doctrines of the Sunnis) and the community (as doctrines and jurisprudence of the Sunni Arab majority), while being wary of the relationship with Sunni Islamic political trends, as well as discussing the possibility of coexistence between Sunni Arab political forces and Kurdish political forces plus the political forces close to Iran, without a coup or violent change.

If the bilateral setup of President Muhammad Al-Halbousi and Sheikh Khamis Al-Khanjar is united, it could create a political symbolism that has the ability to accommodate consensual democracy with a liberal approach as a general climate for Sunni, religious and non-religious forces that want to participate in political activities within the framework of the structure of the new political system, peacefully and without violence. The bilateral alliance between these two sides will help answer a number of questions, namely: How can religious and non-religious political forces establish a dominant political symbolism somewhat similar to the symbolism of the Kurdish political house able to compete in the liberal climate of the state to reach a partnership commensurate with the weight of the masses of those parties electorally in the ruling? What are the most important manifestations of this union or alliance and its features? When and how did liberal Iraqi Sunni Arab symbolism emerge? Are consensual democracy and the liberal system the only healthy climate from which Arab Sunni forces can breathe?

Finally, can the Sunni Forces Alliance be considered in the organizational sense that we used to talk about the coalitions of the Kurdish political house? Or it is a liberal alliance that used pragmatic tactics which would not lead it to the formation of a strategic alliance through which a building of Sunni Arab political symbolism that controls the governorates of the Sunni Arab majority can be achieved.

If the bilateral coalition of Al-Halbousi and Al-Khanjar succeeds, its manifestations may emerge as follows:

1.   A new methodology in creating a leading symbolism for (the Sunni political house) and the process of modifying the position of Sunni representation in government and parliament. The use of the power of the dualism alliance in the reformist expression will dominate the idea of participation for the majority of the component of Sunni in the reform process, that starting from it, more than the domination of the clan or doctrinal ideology.

2.   The bilateral coalition expresses what is called (the Libero-Islamic), which means the formation of a platform that can achieve intellectual pluralism by the majority of Muslim conservatives rather than imposing a religious state. Through such a platform, it will be possible for the Sunni to have equal rights to those gained by their neighborship, Kurds and Shiites, through their Kurdish political house and the

Shiite political house, and it will facilitate the negotiation, understanding and reaching compromises as ways to rule.

3. The supposed bilateral coalition may adopt the concept of conservative-liberal democracy, which is a political and social system that reconciles liberalism and religion on the one hand and democratic and national values on the one hand. It rejects the political discourse based on dualities that impose a monochromic political vision, separatism, or hard-line religious practices that eliminate the rest.

4. The supposed alliance of the existing political system presents three achievements:

   a. Decentralization in transferring powers to provinces with a Sunni Arab majority and relieving pressure on the central government by separating the boundaries and tasks of the federal government and local governments.

   b. Consolidating moderate discourse, empowering democracy, and achieving transitional and social justice.

   c. The multiplicity of sources of income and the federal economy provided by local governments in those governorates, as they have an agricultural and industrial economy, large mineral, gas and oil resources, human resources, and multiple experiences. (https://al-akhbar.com)

The Sunni parties bear the greatest burden in the arrival of the Shiites to power in Iraq. If they dealt with the new reality and the political facts produced by the fall of the former regime after 2003 with an open political mentality, and participated in the political process and took the initiative in building Iraqi society on the basis of democratic principles and the provisions of the constitution, the situation would not be as it is now, which turned in favour of political parties, including the Sunni parties, monopolized the power and extended their control over all state institutions. These Sunni parties committed two fatal strategic mistakes, the first of which was: they rejected the new changed political reality altogether and stood firmly against it in a desperate attempt to turn the clock back ... of course, this is impossible. And the second is when the Sunni forces were preoccupied with confronting the American occupation, expelling the invading forces, jihad, national and popular resistance, and preparing the Iraqi Sunni public opinion against it, the Shiites were marching towards power and controlling its joints calmly, but steadily and resolute, and within a short period they were able to form a large security force from army and police that reached million people. This force later became a tool for striking the opposition in the Sunni provinces, crushing their sit-ins and protests, eradicating them. After getting rid of the Sunni resistance, this regular sectarian force supported by Iran may turn to confront the forces of the Kurdistan region, the last difficult obstacle to forming their Shiites sectarian state. Since the first day of the regime change in Iraq, the Shiites have demanded the position of prime minister by claiming that they represent the majority of the population in the country. Such a claim was not valid as no single census conducted in Iraq since 2003. It was important to conduct a census before the two parliamentary elections (2005 and 2010) to find out the allocation ratio of parliamentary seats for each component depending on the number of Iraq's population, but it was ignored. Moreover, although the Sunni Iraqi List won in the 2010 elections 91 seats in Parliament, the Shiite coalition of Dawlat Al Qannon, led by Nuri al-Maliki, was considered the winner of the election despite the fact that it had 89 seats only. Nevertheless, their insistence on obtaining the premiership stemmed from their false claim that they are the majority. Therefore that was considered as the biggest trick that affected the Sunni parties and blocs, including the Kurds. Based on this claim, it seems that the Shiites will win the premiership even if they do not win any seat in the Parliament. Of course, these dangerous political developments would not have occurred in Iraq if the Sunni parties had participated in the ongoing political process and did not take positions hostile to the new political situation.

And the second fatal mistake committed by the Sunni Islamic and nationalist forces, among the many mistakes that the Iraqi people still pay for, is that it showed violent hostility to the Kurds and Kurdish parties, especially the Islamic party affiliated with the Muslim Brotherhood-led by the Vice President of the Republic accused of terrorism, Tariq al-Hashemi, and everyone witnessed how the majority of the Iraqi Sunni List deputies withdrew from the parliament hall, in protest against the election of Jalal Talabani as president of Iraq in 2010 because he was from the Kurdish component. And those Sunni parties, regardless of their intellectual and ideological diversity, still view the Kurds as the first enemy of Iraq, and their legitimate nationalist projects must be faced. This is happening while al-Maliki is waging a fierce military campaign against Sunni cities, and it is assumed, politically and ideologically, that the two Sunni Arab and Kurdish components will seek an alliance between them to stand in the face of their common enemy. However, the inherited Arab racial intolerance prevented this from happening, despite the Kurdistan region and its leadership is sheltering many Sunni leaders fleeing the oppression and persecution of al-Maliki, such as Tariq al-Hashemi and other leaders of the Sunni sit-ins in Anbar province. Mishaan Al-Jubouri, as one of the former members of Sunni Arab, has initiated his election program by calling on Iraqis to liberate Iraq from the Kurdish occupation. This mentality prevails in the Sunni political milieu in Iraq. The balance of power in Iraq could have tilted in favour of the Sunni Arab and Kurdish component if the two parties had agreed on a unified strategy to confront Al-Maliki's expansionist ambitions, but the blind racial hatred is shown by the Sunni Arabs towards the Kurds and their attempt to undermine their legitimate national gains prompted the Kurds to support the Shiite parties in taking overruling in the hope that something will be accomplished for their cause. They were wrong and did not manage to achieve any right or wrong thing from it, just as the Sunni Arabs lost before when they boycotted the elections and turned hostile towards the Kurds. The only one who won everything and lost nothing is the Shiite parties. [makkahnewspaper.com]

Kurdish Parties Sultanate and Tails

The system of government in the Kurdistan region is based on family and tribal hegemony (Barzaniya and Talabania), practising cronyism, relatives' protection, and commitment to blood ties away from national responsibility, professional competence, job experience, democratic, legal, and cultural application. As the Iraqi society is politically, economically, and security unstable, this sultanic Aghawati regime strengthens the values of adherence and protection to it, so it was used against those demanding the democratic system, respect for citizenship and political awareness, and this is what the Kurdistan Democratic Party and the Patriotic Union of Kurdistan did. The networks of patronage, which led to the consolidation of the foundations of the sultanic system, resulted in the transformation of the former revolutionaries into businessmen that led to the demise of the borders and the separation between the political and economic classes. Therefore, the Barzani and Talabani families held the best government positions, so they monopolized the economy, the security services, the police, and the peshmerga, and they controlled the media. This means that the economic boom and political transformations did not lead to the distribution of economic and political power among the Kurds in general. Rather, it was confined to the hands of the men of the two ruling families of the

Kurdish region. This means that the economic boom and political transformations did not lead to the distribution of economic and political power among the Kurds in general. Rather, it was confined to the hands of the men of the two ruling families of the Kurdish region. And the urban boom has aggravated the situation and achieved severe disparities between the rich and the poor, in line with the spread of corruption at the highest levels, distorting the market and inflating prices, forcing the commoners to work more than one job in order to cover living expenses. It goes without saying that the basis of the Kurdish parties is feudal groupings that have nothing to do with reform and the freedom struggle because they practice extortion, arrogance, and exploitation of circumstances in order to slash the largest piece of Iraq, so they became businessmen and then financial gangs while remaining with the mentality of the families of the inherited tribal. They aspire and personal and family goals that are deceiving and devoid of principles, so feudalism and wealthy people became the source of the inherited power. They do not have a comprehensive development project; they rely on the Americans and the Israeli in their empowering and support. These feudal parties have an invisible or deep corrupt state in Kurdistan hiding under a network of politicians, businessmen, and media institutions ready to buy up the cheap writers and journalists who do not have principles, with unclean conscience, lack of talent and the brilliant. These parties are:-

1.   Kurdistan Islamic Union.

2.   The Patriotic Union of Kurdistan.

3.   The Kurdistan National Alliance.

4.   The Islamic Group in Kurdistan.

5.   The Kurdistan Socialist Democratic Party.

6.   The Kurdistan Revolutionary Party.

7.   The Kurdistan Democratic Party.

8.   Movement of change.

9.   The New Generation Movement.

They are national-ethnic parties that do not include all nationalities and ethnicities in Iraq and do not represent organizations that mediate between the Kurds and Iraqis or the government, but they are non-sectarian. They have their own army called the Peshmerga and security force Assayas. The Barzani Democratic Party is characterized by authority over the region, and the small Kurdish parties have complained about the oppression of authoritarian parties in the region, such as the Change Movement and the New Generation. Some of the pictures of the corruption of the Kurdistan Democratic Party include: -

1.   Oil smuggling and control of customs at border outlets and its absolute domination of border crossings, the oil file, money, and salaries. The other remaining parties that participate in Parliament and

the government have no authority at all, as this party smuggles oil and protects smugglers to Turkey and Iran by about 300 thousand barrels per day from the fields of Kirkuk and the Kurdistan region. In general, the Kurdish parties in particular (Democratic and Union) steal $700 million per month of oil and customs, as well as steal nearly $200 million per month from the border crossings. No one knows where this money is going. Not only that, but Kurdish government figures also steal grants allocated to needy families and register them for their own account (this is one of the crimes of the state in Kurdistan).

2. Cheap sexual intelligence blackmails of Iraqi political figures in order to dominate the Ministry of Finance, embassies, and important state institutions. The worst of all types of Kurdish corruption now is the Kurdish parties are extorting immoral acts of the Shiite leaders through videotaped recordings of the exposed sexual situations of these (Shiite leaders) in order to blackmail them into accepting conditions that the Kurdish parties put on them in an explosive and silent file including the insistence of the Kurdish parties running the Ministry of Finance as it is important in empowering the Mafia's hegemony, as

well as their hegemony over jobs in the diplomatic corps in embassies and some important institutions.

3. The monopoly of the economy in the hands of the ruling families (Barzanis and Talabanis), where businessmen who seek to obtain government contracts pay 10-30% of the contract value and become partners to the company owned by one of the party sponsors, plus another 19% to the director of the government department that issues the contract.

4. Monopolising the market in an integrated way and linking local parties and families through economic conglomerates such as the Deyaar Group, the Falcon Group, the KAR Group, the Nasri Group, the Sandy Group and the Silver Star Group, which covers many economic sectors.

5. Buying the votes of voters with money: the Kurdistan Democratic Party pays salaries to thousands of citizens from the regions of Kurdistan, Halabja and Sayed Sadiq in exchange for voting to the party in every parliamentary election in the Iraqi parliament or the regional parliament.

6. The Kurdistan Democratic Party has introduced 350,000 Kurds (Turkish, Iranian and Syrian) to the Kurdistan Regional Authority within the region's population records, and they receive salaries from the public budget. The majority of them reside in the

143

border province of Dohuk with Turkey in order to exploit their votes in the elections after granting them citizenship without obtaining government approval in Baghdad.

7. Transforming the Kurdistan Democratic Party and the Patriotic Union of Kurdistan from yesterday's revolutionaries into today businessmen and financial gangs.

8. The use of the Peshmerga to defend the rule of the two families. It also supported the American and British invading forces in Iraq in March 2003. After the fall of Saddam Hussein, it assumed full responsibility for security in the Kurdish region and participated with the US army in most of its operations inside Iraq.

9. In the areas under its administration, the Democratic Party prohibited any demonstrations, whatever their cause. However, thousands of Kurds demonstrated in Sulaymaniyah against the local authorities due to widespread corruption, poor basic services, cuts to salaries for employees, as well as unemployment of university graduates, so they expressed their discontent and dissatisfaction with the rule of the two families for them. My comment on the above is: if the rule is democratic, why the demonstrations and protests in Sulaymaniyah? Why is there an army that

protects the rule of the two families? And why are there secret prisons? Why are the Iraqi government politicians and Shiite figures blackmailed by the Kurdistan Democratic Party in a cheap and dirty manner? So, they are parties that are not intermediaries between the people and the government, and the employees of the two parties are practising white-collar crimes and tribal crimes dominated by the feudal tribal mentality. Their parties reinforce authoritarianism, spread corruption, impoverish millions of Kurds, and widen the gap between the government and the people, which means the corrupt control over the joints of government administrations. In addition to the above, the region suffers from high inflation, unemployment, interruption of basic services and the waste of public money by officials close to Masoud Barzani. Therefore, the general Kurds sought to demand democracy and remove the sultanate system through the application of the rule of law, merit, transparency, and accountability.

After this introduction, we provide some articles that explain what we came up with, namely:

1. Chronic Corruption in The Federal Kurdistan Region:

After the Gulf War in March 1991, two no-fly zones were imposed; The northern no-fly zone operated north of the 36th parallel for the Kurds protection in April 1991, and the southern no-fly zone operated south of the 32nd parallels for the Shiite's protection in August 1992. The two regions were separated by the Centre where Baghdad, the capital, is and hence the powers of Saddam Hussein's regime have been reduced to the Sunni Baathist cities. The goal, as announced, is the immediate cessation of Saddam Hussein's brutal repression of the Kurds and Shiites, as stipulated in Security Council Resolution No. 688 of 1991. As a result of the hardening of the Baath-chauvinist position of Kurdish demands, all the administrative and military state institutions were withdrawn from the governorates of Sulaymaniyah, Arbil and Dohuk. The leaders of the Kurdish parties had shared the influence and imports, and their eye was first on the machines, mechanisms, bulldozers, and cars in Bikhama Dam to confiscate and sell them. The Kurdistan Regional Government was established in 1992 to fill the vacuum caused by the withdrawal of Baghdad's administrative authorities, and then the party leaders seized vast lands, cities and palaces of the Baath leaders and buildings as headquarters for their parties and families, and they are still living in them, and their properties have expanded to

146

unprecedented limits. People have been forced to live under the killing economic blockade by the Baghdad government, which itself is subject to UN Security Council sanctions. The living conditions for the majority of the people were unbearably difficult. The heads of the Kurdish parties - a heterogeneous mixture of familial, tribal, religious, and nationalist tendencies - believed that Saddam Hussein was still powerful, and they continued to communicate with him more often in secret and less in public. They reached a tribal reconciliation with him to turn the page of the past and complete silence with regard to the thousands of Barzanis who were exterminated in 1983. After his defeat in 1991 in Kuwait, Saddam Hussein had revived the tribal neighbourhoods, which was cancelled by the 14th July 1958 revolution, to solve disputes between citizens. The Kurdish leaders who returned from across the border were carrying their grudges, intentions, and old revolts, and the corruption that accompanied them in the sixties and first half of the seventies remained intrinsic to them and even increased as a result of the Iranian government imposing some controls on them between the years 1975-1991, which do not allow them exercising the absolute power. Between the years 1991-2003, when they returned from Iran, their aspirations were reduced to the level of building secret relations with Saddam Hussein's intelligence, trading with Qusay and Uday, monopolizing Ibrahim al-Khalil's customs imports, and

147

secretly receiving money and weapons from Baghdad. In 1994, the conflict erupted between them over money and influence into internal battles, and Saddam Hussein supported one party closer to him against the other. And he would be generous to the extent of sending tank units to support his loyalists, who are the leaders of the Kurdistan Democratic Party, in the leadership war that was raging throughout Kurdistan and in Erbil in particular. More than 3,000 combatants and civilians were killed in this war, and tens of thousands were displaced. from 1991 until the collapse of the Baath regime in 2003, the heads of the Kurdish parties were the de facto authority in the three governorates, Sulaymaniyah, Erbil and Dohuk. The Power was concentrated in the hands of the ruling families that owned parties and were working to perpetuate a non-democratic system closer to a clan system, in which the tribe's leader had absolute powers. In 1998, the United States called on them to stop their internal battles. Accordingly, the KDP and the PUK formed two competing governments. After the fall of Saddam Hussein's regime in 2003, the influential in the leadership of the two parties concluded what was called a strategic agreement in 2007, which was, in fact, a deal between two leaders to share power and wealth while the old animosity at the bipartisan level remained frozen, out of concern for their financial shares. The two sides agreed on a 50/50 split for the region rule.

Yesterday's revolutionaries turned into businessmen and then into financial gangs active at home and abroad. A telegram issued by the US State Department in 2006, published by WikiLeaks, stating that "corruption is the biggest economic problem in Kurdistan," and it provided interesting details about favouritism in the region. In a 2008 BBC report, a businessman describes corruption in Kurdistan: is a virus telling the reporter: "It is killing Kurdistan". Perhaps one of the most important features of the behaviour of most Kurdish party leaders is the subordination of politics to financial interests and the publicity of Kurdish national rights. And the constant need for an external protector, Saddam Hussein was the back, and after his fall, they met his replacement, Mr Rejab Tayyib Erdogan, and still is. As of mid-2013, there were 2,656 registered foreign companies from 80 countries in the region; Turkey's share was 1226 companies. The food security of the region is in the hands of Turkey, as the regional government neglected the development of the agricultural sector, dairy production, handicrafts and local tissues, and people relied entirely on imported materials and goods. As a result of the dishonest dealings with Baghdad, Ankara played a greater role, not Erbil, over the energy sector in the Kurdistan region and related revenues. Politically, the relationship with Turkey empowered the KDP's grip on power and, to a lesser extent, the Patriotic

Union of Kurdistan. Turkey's goal was not only to turn the region into a region of its economic dependence but also to achieve political gains by marketing the Kurdistan Democratic Party and its president as an alternative political model for the PKK and its leader Abdullah Ocalan, as well as using its president as a pressure card on the Baghdad government! When Saddam Hussein's regime was overthrown in 2003, the Shiite opposition returned from abroad - some of them from Baathist backgrounds, who rebelled against him later - and the leaders of the Kurdish parties preceded them 12 years in return, and they were proficient in practising corruption and spoiling, rigging all elections and selling oil and its derivatives through Borders illegally and across the dark scenes in the interest of a certain number of members of the ruling family. Officials admitted that between 2004 and 2010, the KDP and the Patriotic Union of Kurdistan each received $35 million a month in public funds to fund their parties. The total of these sums amounted to about $ 5 billion over a period of six years, which represents approximately 20 per cent of the general budget annually. Party leaders also used public funds to fund more than 400 parallel and party-supported media outlets. Party media and parallel media occupy most of the media space in Kurdistan and provide opportunities to purchase large numbers of journalists as mercenaries whose mission is to inject lies for the benefit of the ruling family and numb

150

collective consciousness in society, the personality cult of some of the leaders, and providing misleading propaganda for both parties. The engineer of chaos (Paul Bremer) had a negative view of the Arab and Kurdish elites, and he was the engineer who shaped the post-Saddam Hussein regime. It is evident from what he wrote that the loss of immunity to financial temptations: "The indolent work was an obstacle to the effectiveness of the Governing Council," and from the two Kurdish leaders: "They were unable to agree on who would take the Kurdish seat from them." The leaders of the two parties requested "large financial grants" from the central treasury, and in this regard, Bremer recalls: "We have provided the Kurds with some face-saving options regarding financial grants." He says: "The only issue that was quickly resolved in the Governing Council was determining the salaries of its members" ... I reached an outrageous budget for the Council ... Bremer continues, "I informed the council that the budget that they proposed for the 25 members exceeds the budget of the Ministry of Education, which includes more than 325,000 employees.". It must be noted that the Shiite leaders did not act with Saddam Hussein's regime as the Kurdish leaders did, so they did not give in or negotiate. They insisted on the fall of the regime, and they returned from abroad after the US occupation of Iraq. The hostility was intense against the Shiite leaders returning from abroad, and they assassinated Mr Abdul Majeed Al-Khoei and Mr Muhammad Baqir Al-Hakim. Abdul Zahra Othman, the last man to assume the presidency of the Interim Governing Council and from the Da'wa Party, has also been assassinated. Successive ministries were formed after the Transitional Governing Council: Headed by Iyad Allawi, Ibrahim al-Jaafari, Nuri al-Maliki, Haider al-Abadi and now Adel Abdul-Mahdi. There was a variation in the performance of the roles, a decrease, or an increase in the size of corruption according to the personality of the prime minister and the extent of commitment to the principles and the internal, regional and international political circumstances in which he worked, and their conditions were very difficult. And what takes on the governments of Baghdad to turn a blind eye to the embezzlement and waste of public money by the Kurdish leadership and not to listen to the complaints of the Kurdish people, which raises the question of the possibility of a mutual understanding?! There is no doubt that this indifferent position was a green light to consolidate the foundations of the Kleptocracy, a government composed of corrupt leaders stealing the wealth of their people and defrauding the rule of law. There is no doubt that the social environment in which the leaders of the Kurdish parties exercised their power was safer, and the Ba'athists did not have popularity or influence among the Kurdish population, as was the case in the central and southern cities of Iraq. The president of (Hadak) established relations of understanding on several levels with the regime of Saddam Hussein and did not abandon them until after his regime collapsed, Whereas the Baathists focused their hatred on the Shiite leaders wherever they were, and they fought the occupation forces in revenge for their loss of the privileges they enjoyed during their unjust and authoritarian rule. The conditions of Kurdish society were more ready to adopt civil society institutions, democratic practice, and respect for the rule of law. However, the essence of the leaders of the parties - which are heavily armed parties - are prisoners of the inherited tribal mentality, where their aspirations and their personal and family goals are devoid of principles. The rampant corruption in Kurdistan is not foreign or strange, but It is the result of the long feudal era in Kurdish society, where (the Agha) is the source of power, and he bequeaths it to his children, and no one is entitled to question him. The authority of the Aghas in the Badinan regions in the fifties and sixties of the last century was a witness to the pattern of rule outside the law. These Aghas are widespread, and they were known as a gang of thieves in Badinan for more than a century. The leaders of today's parties are the children and grandchildren of those Aghas, and they have adapted to the national rights of the Kurdish people to preserve their interests and privileges, which are no longer viable for the blatant feudal ideology. From here, they changed their masks and covered themselves by the mantle of nationalism and the

Kurdish state. The descendants of these Aghas today are masters of Badinan, and many of them were Saddam Hussein's mercenaries and participants in his crimes against the Kurdish people! These are the beneficiaries of corruption and spoil and stand against any attempt to change the status quo. In confronting them, the Kurdish people failed in their struggle for democracy, building the foundations of a solid national economy, forming an army and a unified security apparatus free from partisan and family restrictions, and their loyalty to the people and the homeland and not to a handful of party leaders and their entourage. It is naive to imagine that post-Bremer leaders can introduce radical political reforms in the style of governance and stop corruption among party leaders and their relatives. This results from their feeling of the fragility of the ground on which they stand and the depth of the contradictions between the interests of party leaders and the political process subject to bargaining and consensus between families the influential people. In fact, they do not have a comprehensive development project and a desire for personal wealth. All this leads to the death of laws and circumvention of them. The first step in the right direction begins with a comprehensive dialogue between Arabs, Kurds, and all other components to build a unified political movement that gives priority to combating corruption throughout Iraq, starting with (Erbil and Baghdad). This is possible provided that the

154

loyalty and the jealousy for the interest of the people and the country are at the forefront goals of the elite that adopts the project. [https://xeber24.org].

2.   **Corruption of the rule of Kurdish family in the region:**

The crisis of financial corruption that ravages the body of the region and swallows its wealth prompted some politicians opposed to the Authority Party to accuse Massoud Barzani and his family of corruption. A member of the Islamic Group in the region's parliament, Suzan Omar, revealed that there are 14 files related to corruption and waste of money cases by the region's president, the head of the Kurdistan party, and some close to among them is Masrour Barzani. Senior officials in the region accuse Masoud Barzani and his ruling family of being involved in financial corruption cases and amassing a huge fortune for his family instead of serving the people of the region. Masrour Barzani, the son of Masoud and his nephew Nechirvan Barzani, acquires companies and economic investments, most notably the communications company Korek, where he commissioned its establishment $ 600 million and media channels with huge budgets, such as Rudaw, owned by Nechirvan, and Masrour's satellite channel 24K. An American magazine recently revealed in a report that Mansour, the son of Masoud Barzani, bought two palaces in Beverly Hills for $47 million paid in cash, a topic

155

that caught the attention of the American press, as clear evidence of the extent of rampant corruption in the ruling families in the region. While Shaswar AbdulWahid, head of the (New Generation) movement, revealed information that the two Kurdish parties' revenues from the border crossings amounted to $200 million per month and confirmed that the primary responsibility in plundering the region's wealth falls on the Democratic Party and the Patriotic Union, indicating that Masrour Barzani smuggled oil illegally cross the border and sold it to Turkish traders and transferred the other part of the oil to Israel, a scandal which its details is known to the leaders of the two Kurdish parties. He confirmed that sales revenues are recorded in special bank accounts for what he claims to be the oil minister in the region (Ashti Hawrami) and in private accounts in the names of Barzani's family in Turkish and European banks without recording it as the region's financial revenues which must be transferred to the central treasury in Baghdad. The corruption crisis in the Kurdistan region is not limited to smuggling oil and controlling institutions but also includes the fictitiously affiliated jobs in the joints of government departments. Mrs Hasina Ke Reddy, a member of Parliament, revealed that the corrupt Kurdistan Democratic Party and the fictitiously affiliated jobs to it have plundered the people's wealth and destroyed the region over the past years. She says (Ke Reddy) that there are 86 thousand people who receive from one to five salaries and that 152 people have finished their service with the rank of a minister and receive a pension without any of them holding a ministerial position in the local government of the region. And the special grades receive ID5 million monthly salaries from the government. Also, there are more than 101 thousand people who receive more than one salaries, 55 thousand from which are fictitiously affiliated employees to steal public money, excluding railway employees whose number is 32 employees, most of them are staff of the two Kurdish parties though the region does not have a train. The reality is that the formality procedures for prosecuting the corrupt in the region are limited to junior employees, while the corrupt senior members of the Barzani family, merchants, brokers, and organizers of illusory deals are not approached by them, and they are above the law. It seems that the partisan immunity enjoyed by the leaders and high grads staff of the two parties is one of the reasons for the failure to eliminate corruption and the corrupt from the political layer in the region. Simply because whoever enjoys power, money, influence, protection, immunity, and party support, and earns several salaries in a month, is not subject to the anti-corruption law. This confirms that corruption and tyranny in the region are not better than the situation in the rest of Iraq, especially since the Kurds of the Kurdistan region have been suffering for years from political tyranny, corruption, and injustice due to the authority of the two families of the two Kurdish parties. This is clearly showing that the region's economic and social success story was nothing but an illusion that will not continue for long in facing the facts on the ground. [https://aliraqnews.com]

3.   **The Politicized Society in Kurdistan Faces Sultanistic Regime**:

The political economy of the Kurdish sultanate is based on economic monopolies and patronage networks, which are being used to enrich the ruling elites in the region co-opt some sectors of society and contain the opposition. While the lack of transparency and accountability makes it difficult to obtain accurate and credible data, some former opposition groups, which are now part of the government, local and international media and WikiLeaks have been able to highlight these practices. For example, the US State Department telegram in 2006, published by WikiLeaks, considered corruption "the biggest economic problem in Kurdistan" and provided interesting details about cronyism in the region. According to the document, titled "Corruption in the Kurdish North," businessmen seeking government contracts pay 10-30 per cent of the contract value to become "partners" of the company owned by a party sponsor, and another 10 per cent to the Director of the government department that issues the contract. The telegram mentions several conglomerates by name, including the Deyaar

Group, the Falcon Group, the KAR Group, the Nasri Group, the Sandy Group, and the Silver Star Group, which cover many sectors, and thus monopolize the market in an integrated manner and are linked to the ruling local parties and families. The devastating long-term impact of corruption on the Kurdish economy and society was demonstrated by a BBC report in 2008, in which a businessman openly tells a reporter that relatives of political leaders "may get a government job with a budget or contract, for example, "They might get a government job with a budget or a contract, for example, of $1 million or $2 million to rebuild a road. According to the reporter, "It did not matter whether this person was able to actually build a road". The contract is repeatedly sold until it reaches a real construction company. At that time, there may only be half of the money left. The businessman likened corruption to a virus, saying, "It is killing Kurdistan." Kurdish leaders also used their power to earn big salaries, and they oversaw a system in which many other people were generously rewarded to help create their own networks of patronage and ensure the loyalty of their close friends. According to unofficial sources, the Kurdistan Regional Government pays extremely high salaries to officials of the special category, such as the president, prime minister, other ministers, members of parliament, general managers, and advisors. President Masoud Barzani's salary is said to be $ 18,979 per month, while his deputy, Kosrat Rasul Ali, from the Patriotic Union of Kurdistan, gets $ 16,448 a month. It is believed that the salary and allowances of the former Iraqi president and leader of the Patriotic Union of Kurdistan, Jalal Talabani, amount to one million dollars a year, and perhaps much more. The federal government pays the salaries and allocations of Kurdish officials in Baghdad, but it is deducted from the region's share of 17 per cent annually, and thus it constitutes a great burden on the general budget. In addition to the high salaries and allowances for special employees, the Kurdistan Regional Government spends approximately $ 717 million a month, or between 70 and 80 per cent of the general budget, on salaries and retirement benefits for the 1.4 million people described as civil servants. By providing jobs and public benefits to the population, the KDP and the Patriotic Union of Kurdistan aim to monitor and suppress public dissent. While accurate data is not available, there may be 100,000 employees who are paid two salaries, some are paid but are not working, and others receive illegal pensions. In addition, the territorial government provides high salaries, pensions, land, jobs, and admission to universities for special category officials, their children and their relatives, and others with ties to both parties. According to a study conducted by Change Movement (Gouran) in 2014, which is the second-largest party and was previously in the opposition ranks, from 2000 to 2010, hundreds of people were appointed and retired legally and illegally, on the basis that they are special category officials, while some of them have never worked in these jobs. According to the Change Movement (Gouran), billions of dollars have been paid out to these officials. In the province of Sulaymaniyah, the stronghold of the Patriotic Union of Kurdistan, the Public Prosecutor reported in March 2014 that an investigation concluded that the region's president or prime minister had referred to retirement 158 people as officials in the special category with monthly pensions of $ 258,000, although these people did not actually take over those jobs. In the regional parliament, which consists of 111 members, there are 55 "advisers", each of whom receives approximately $ 4,700 a month. It has been reported that the Presidency of Parliament wants to reform the list of chancellors. There are countless other examples. According to the head of the Parliamentary Committee for Human Rights in the Kurdistan Regional Government, the Kurdistan Democratic Party, through the General Directorate of Pensions, referred 27,000 people to retirement as veterans before the elections that took place in 2013, in an attempt to obtain votes. A report issued in 2014 indicated that the KDP and the PUK had appointed 1,437 people as teachers and employees in the city of Khanaqin since 2003, 200 of whom worked part-time, while the others never came to work. The Ministry of Education is said to have paid them a total of $860,000 monthly "salaries". Kurdish officials also receive remunerative salaries for their work in Baghdad. It is believed that the total amount of salaries and allowances received by Kurdish officials in the federal government and the national parliament from 2003 to 2013 reached an astronomical figure of one billion dollars. The federal government withdraws this amount from the 17 per cent of the annual national budget that goes to the Kurdistan Regional Government. In the absence of a party financing law, the KDP and the PUK have also used the general budget to finance partisan activities, as well as parallel and party-supported media outlets. After pressure from the previous opposition, which is now part of the government, which consists of the Change Movement (Gouran), the Kurdistan Islamic Union, the Islamic Group in Kurdistan (Komali Islami), and from civil society, officials admitted that between 2004 and 2010, Kurdistan Democratic Party and Patriotic Union of Kurdistan have each received $35 million a month from the public funds to fund their two parties. The total of these sums reached about 5 billion dollars over a period of six years. which represents approximately 20 per cent of the general budget annually. In addition, the two parties used public funds to finance more than 400 parallel and party-supported media outlets, while the few independent media outlets and those associated with the former opposition did not receive such funding. Party-supported media and parallel media occupy most of the media space in Kurdistan, provide job opportunities for journalists, participate in co-opting each other, reinforce the personality cult of some leaders, provide propaganda for both parties, shape and influence public opinion, attack each other, and attack other parties and independent media.

Structural Weaknesses and Dynamic Processes

Despite the success of the KDP and the Patriotic Union of Kurdistan in establishing and consolidating the foundations of the sultanic system, this system suffers from structural and organic weaknesses. In addition, its internal development is much more vital than it appears. This situation could (unintentionally) provide opportunities for reforms, the emergence of new political and social groups, a torn off sultanic system, and a more pluralistic political landscape. If these potential changes do not lead to instability and infighting, they will benefit the democratic development in the region. At the same time, the system's primary strengths, namely personality and lineage, are its greatest weaknesses. This is because the centre of the sultanic system is the leader, not the institutions. While the KDP and the Patriotic Union of Kurdistan control state institutions, decisions are made on the basis of the leader's personal whims rather than through those institutions. Both parties suffer from serious succession struggles that threaten their internal cohesion and unity. The shape and scale of any potential change in the two parties will vary based on their different structures and backgrounds.

The Kurdistan Democratic Party (KDP): more centralized and institutional than the Patriotic Union of

Kurdistan, and thus long ago acted as a sultanic party. The KDP describes itself as a national liberation movement and has been led by the Barzani family since its founding in 1946. KDP officials are clear and frank about the fact that the party cannot be separated from the Barzani family. However, while the KDP cadres and voters accept the Barzani dynasty, this does not mean that they approve of corruption by high-level officials. Although Masoud Barzani is the undisputed leader of the KDP, the struggle of the wings exists within the party. There is a power struggle between his eldest son and the Security Council advisor, Masrour Barzani, and Prime Minister Nechirvan Barzani (Masoud's nephew) over who should succeed Barzani, the father, at the head of the party. There is little public information available about Massoud Barzani's position on this issue, so it is difficult to predict how the internal rivalry will develop. The appointment of two Kurdish leaders to senior positions in the new government in Baghdad in late 2014 illustrates the divisions plaguing the KDP. Initially, Roche Nuri Shaways was appointed Minister of Finance, while Hoshyar Zebari was named Deputy Prime Minister. Shaways refused to be finance minister. Masoud Barzani is alleged to have supported Zebari as deputy prime minister, while Nechirvan is said to have supported Shaways to take the post. Ultimately, Shaways was appointed deputy prime minister. Perhaps deepening these divisions is the fact that influential politicians in the KDP and the Patriotic Union of Kurdistan own private media and paramilitary forces. Powerful politicians use the media to talk about their own factions, criticize others, influence public opinion, and attract young journalists from independent and opposition media by providing high salaries, career advancement opportunities, and other benefits, such as free housing. The polarization in the media is reinforced by the absence of an independent national television channel. Aside from the flank struggle, the KDP is facing a deep crisis in its popularity and identity, says pro-KDP journalist Rebwar Wali. New and empowered leaders are not being prepared, most KDP Politburo members focus on their commercial activities rather than politics, and political and cultural reforms in the party are generally not implemented. Meanwhile, there are protests against corruption and human rights violations in the KDP strongholds in Dohuk and Erbil. People have become more confident in expressing their discontent through social media and street protests. However, there are two factors that constitute an obstacle to the increase in opposition in terms of quantity and quality. First, the suppression of the KDP prevents people in Dohuk and Erbil from increasing opposition, as is the case in the areas of the Patriotic Union of Kurdistan. The second obstacle is the conservative nature of Erbil and Dohuk compared to the more liberal and progressive Sulaymaniyah. These difficulties make the

166

issues of succession and the future of the KDP in the post-Masoud Barzani era less predictable than it might seem. Shifts and generational changes at the leadership level are likely to produce new dynamics and lead to positive changes in the political system.

The Patriotic Union of Kurdistan: which is the other power in Kurdistan, defines itself as a social-democratic party. Its founders sought to establish a modern party as an alternative to the KDP, which they considered conservative and reactionary. However, after thirty-nine years, the Patriotic Union of Kurdistan has become similar to the Kurdistan Democratic Party. The Patriotic Union of Kurdistan consists of three factions, the strongest of which is headed by Talabani's wife and member of the Political Bureau, Hiro Ibrahim Ahmed. Despite claims to the contrary, this faction aims to consolidate the power of the Talabani family. This was evident in June 2014, when Qubad Talabani, the younger son of Jalal Talabani, was appointed deputy prime minister in the Kurdistan Regional Government. This appointment violated an important rule of the Patriotic Union of Kurdistan party, which says that the candidate for this sensitive position must be a member of the political bureau, and Qubad is not a member of it and met with great opposition from some members of the office. Members of the Talabani family occupy powerful positions in the party, government, parliament, and security services, and their faction controls many of the party's major blocs and media, as well as managing the party's international relations. However, the family faces major challenges to tighten its grip on the Patriotic Union of Kurdistan party. First, the faction lacks a clear successor to the charismatic founder of the party, Jalal Talabani, who is not disputed. While the family appears to be grooming Qubad to lead the party, he is young and inexperienced and does not have his father's charisma. According to Fred Assard, director of the Kurdistan Center for Strategic Studies, Qubad's chances of leading the party appear slim. Barham Salih and Kosrat Rasul Ali lead the second and third factions in the party. Saleh's faction has tried to be more assertive in its criticism of Talabani's faction, and it is said that it wants to establish a satellite television station to promote its views. Because of the discord and the lack of a clear person to be its next leader, the Patriotic Union of Kurdistan indefinitely postponed holding a conference to choose a successor to Jalal Talabani. Other constant weaknesses, despite the reunification of the separate party administrations that ruled Kurdistan until 2006, the basic components of the security services, peshmerga, police, and financial institutions remain divided along party lines. The influential leaders of both the KDP and the Patriotic Union of Kurdistan have their own paramilitary forces. This contrasts with the increasing demands of society to establish state institutions and the claims of both parties that they want to build national institutions. Another weakness of the system lies in its dependence on oil revenues, which makes it vulnerable to fluctuations in oil prices, disputes with Baghdad that control how oil money is spent, and dependence on Turkey, which is a major customer in oil sales. These weaknesses have been exacerbated by the neglect of productive sectors such as agriculture. Consequently, this rentier system is unable, in the long run, to respond to the structural needs of diversification of the economy or to the demands of society for an economy that does not depend on nepotism at the expense of the public interest. Economically, the region still relies on the federal budget to pay employees' salaries and provide social services. However, due to disputes over the disputed areas outside the Kurdistan region, such as Kirkuk's export of oil without Baghdad's approval, the federal government withheld at the beginning of 2014 the Kurdistan Regional Government's budget allocations, which helped create an economic crisis in the region that has been continuing since mid-2015. This resulted in delays in paying employees' salaries and stopping development projects. The economic crisis also resulted from mismanagement of the economy in the Kurdistan Regional Government, as banks ran out of liquidity. As a result, the pace of social protests increased. Bankrupt businessmen organized sit-ins and demonstrations for the first time. Had it not been for the war

169

against the Islamic State and the population's need for security in the increasingly volatile region of Iraq, the Middle East and North Africa, the protests would have escalated further, with unforeseen consequences. A small minority of senior officials in both the Patriotic Union of Kurdistan and the Kurdistan Democratic Party (KDP) and the Barzani and Talabani families control the oil sector, with the Barzani family owning the largest share. Activists and former opposition groups, who are now part of the ministry in the regional government, ordinary citizens, and even the Patriotic Union of Kurdistan, have directed most of their criticism and protests to the lack of transparency and accountability regarding oil contracts and revenues. The lack of long-term and real reform in this vital sector will only increase social and political protests and instability. In addition to overall fragility, both parties face a resilient and empowered society with high hopes and demands.

Growing Indignation: Relations between citizens and between the KDP and the Patriotic Union of Kurdistan are slowly but surely being reconfigured. Intellectuals, activists, and journalists in Kurdistan have begun to criticize the domination of the ruling families, as well as corruption and the lack of social and economic justice in the region. This politicized society increasingly defines its demands in terms of political, social, and economic rights. Hardly a day passes without one or more demonstrations and sit-ins calling for transparency, accountability, the rule of law, and improved social services. Indignation and discontent with unprecedented corruption, the legal and illegal provision of high salaries, and the payment of pensions to friends and relatives are the main slogans in most protests. While the Kurds acknowledge the sacrifices made by the Barzani and Talabani families against successive Iraqi regimes, they also view corruption at the highest levels as one of the biggest problems facing their region. Ordinary people of all colours of the economic, political, and social spectrum complain that the main economic conglomerates are owned by members of the Politburo. This dissatisfaction is reflected in the polls. Between 2009 and 2012, the Gallup Institute for the Study of Public Opinion Trends conducted interviews with 1,066 people in Kurdistan, and the results revealed a radical change in the population's perception of the KDP and the Patriotic Union of Kurdistan. During this period, perceptions of corruption have steadily worsened, with 37 per cent of those surveyed in 2009 saying that corruption is widespread, reaching 61 per cent in 2011 and 81 per cent in 2012. The poll showed discontent. It expressed strong feelings towards both the KDP and the Patriotic Union of Kurdistan. It also showed that the people who are aware of citizenship rights have great hopes and demands and that they want transparency and accountability. No action has been taken to tackle corruption at the highest levels since the 2012 poll.

171

Moreover, the worsening economic crisis that the Kurdistan region has faced since December 2013 has led to an increase in social protests. So, there was likely no positive change in the public's perception of corruption. As a sign of the increased awareness of rights across the diverse spectrum of society, protests took place in large and small cities, towns and villages. In some cases, protests took place in provincial cities that were not perceived as beacons of the opposition. For example, in light of the statements of Talabani and a prominent businessman that the number of millionaires has increased dramatically, the Committee for the Protection of Public Interests in the city of Khanaqin organized in December 2013 a campaign under the slogan "How did you earn these millions?" Activists wanted to know the number of millionaires in the governorates of Erbil and Dohuk, which are both strongholds of the KDP, in addition to the 2,900 millionaires in Sulaymaniyah, whom Talabani mentioned. They also demanded that parliament set up a committee to investigate how these millionaires accumulated their fortunes and announce the results to the public. As of mid-2015, parliament had not taken any action. Independent and former opposition media have played a critical role in reporting corruption and human rights violations. In a 2014 report titled "The Mountain of Impunity Crouches on the Chests of Kurdistan Journalists," the New York-based Committee to Protect Journalists painted a very bleak picture of the lack of the rule of law in the Kurdistan region. Compared to the rest of the Middle East, the region has one of the most progressive laws on the press, as well as a law guaranteeing the right to access information. However, these laws have not been implemented, a problem that can be blamed for their lack of enforcement on the system whereby judges are appointed on the basis of their partisan loyalty rather than on the basis of professional merit and independence. Most attacks on critical journalists went unpunished. This was the case with Kawa Garmiani, an investigative journalist and editor-in-chief of the monthly magazine Rail. The magazine published several reports alleging corruption among senior officials of the Patriotic Union of Kurdistan Party, including a member of the Political Bureau, Major General Mahmoud Singhawi. Garmiani was assassinated in December 2013, which sparked widespread protests in Kurdistan and the Kurdish diaspora. Singhawi was considered the main suspect, as reported by the news, and was arrested on charges of murder, but was released soon after due to insufficient evidence and insisted that he did not kill Garmiani. Although Kurdistan has not experienced uprisings like the one that led to regime change elsewhere in the region, it did witness its short Kurdish version of the Arab Spring. On 17th February 2011, protesters, most of whom were young, took to the streets of Sulaymaniyah, inspired by the events that took place in

Tunisia and Egypt, but also as an indirect result of the accumulated discontent with the KDP and the Patriotic Union of Kurdistan. They called the central square in the city, Saray Azadi, the name of Tahrir Square (after Tahrir Square in Cairo), demanding an end to economic monopolies and human rights violations, and calling for the consecration of social and economic justice and the establishment of democracy in the political system. A noticeable feature of this protest movement was that various forces, such as the Change Movement (Gouran), Islamic parties and civil society organized the demonstrations together. Intellectuals have played a crucial role in providing basic ideas about goals, mobilization tactics, and visions for the protest movement. However, some activists criticized the former opposition, which is now part of the government, for dealing with the demonstrations in an opportunistic manner. Nasik Qadir, a spokeswoman for the protesters, said the former opposition lacked a vision and strategic plans. In addition, these groups did not participate in the demonstrations as political parties but rather as individual activists. Kadir criticized the Change Movement (Gouran) for giving Islamist parties too much space to become visible and prominent at the expense of other groups. Demonstrations remained confined to the Sulaymaniyah governorate because the KDP did not allow protests in Erbil or Dohuk. However, despite this, the demonstrations shocked the entire political spectrum. The security forces suppressed the demonstrations on April 19, 2011, killing ten people and wounding more than 500 others. 39 Supporters of the KDP, the Patriotic Union of Kurdistan, and their security forces burned the independent TV channel NRT in Sulaymaniyah and Radio Gouran (affiliated with the radio station). Movement for Change in Erbil. Despite the backlash from the ruling parties, the former opposition and civil society, in a sign of political maturity, insisted that the demonstrations be peaceful. Parliament decided to meet the demands of the demonstrators and passed a resolution calling for the arrest and prosecution of perpetrators of violence. Courts issued arrest warrants for the perpetrators of the KDP and the Patriotic Union of Kurdistan. But neither party met the protesters' demands, and the perpetrators were not brought to justice. One of the most prominent protests against the sultanic regime occurred after members of parliament from the KDP and the Patriotic Union of Kurdistan voted on June 30, 2013, to extend the term of Masoud Barzani's presidency to mid-August 2015. The agreement between the KDP and the PUK and the law stipulated a two-year extension, and Barzani was not allowed to be re-elected. According to the draft constitution passed by parliament in 2009, Barzani was allowed to serve as president for two terms of eight years which he completed in 2013. The extension of Barzani's mandate represented a confrontation between the determination of the KDP, with the support of the Patriotic Union of Kurdistan, to consolidate the power of the Barzani family and the social determination to reject that. The victory was the ally of the Kurdistan Democratic Party. Intellectuals, the media, civil society, and the parliamentary opposition vehemently opposed the illegal and controversial extension in their view. Even quarrels occurred in Parliament over the extension. The KDP and the Patriotic Union of Kurdistan justified the move by saying that the draft constitution first needs to be approved before a new president is elected. However, the opposition and civil society confirmed that the extension is illegal because the draft constitution was submitted through a caretaker government, while a large number of parliament members were absent.

Initial Signs of Change: Growing public dissatisfaction with the status and behaviour of the KDP and the Patriotic Union of Kurdistan is beginning to result in some changes in the administration of the region. One of the most notable changes over the past six years has been the emergence of the Change Movement (Guoran) in 2009 as a powerful opposition party. The Change Movement (Gouran) won 25 seats in parliament in 2009, although it does not have a strong party system, which shows the strong discontent of some segments of society towards the KDP and the Patriotic Union of Kurdistan. The Change Movement (Gouran) provided a platform for a young generation of activists who do not have support and do not have family ties with the parties to engage in political life and enter parliament in Baghdad, the regional government in Erbil and local governments. In addition, the party enabled civil society and the two Islamist parties in Kurdistan to become more vocal in their criticism of the sultanic regime. However, the Change Movement (Gouran) was unable to communicate and engage with critical voices in Dohuk, the stronghold of the KDP. This is partly due to the repression practised by the KDP, and in the other part because the Change Movement (Gouran) did not have a mobilization strategy that addresses the local conservative environment in Dohuk. Moreover, the change movement (Gouran) focused mainly on political changes and ignored worsening social problems, such as the increase in social violence, violence against women, and the disintegration of the family. It also did not present a vision for dealing with the Kurds in the disputed areas, who present nationalist demands on the federal Iraqi government. Pressures exerted by the former opposition, civil society, and within the Patriotic Union of Kurdistan prompted the Patriotic Union of Kurdistan and the Kurdistan Democratic Party, in principle, to end their 2007 strategic agreement on the division of wealth and jobs in Kurdistan and Baghdad, and to participate together in the elections. This caused a return to competition in the electoral process and benefited the democratic development in Kurdistan. Although the change did not directly weaken the two main political forces in Kurdistan, it demonstrated the importance of civil and political pressure aimed at weakening an agreement that symbolizes the joint effort of both parties to consolidate the sultanic system. After years of constant pressure from the former opposition and civil society, parliament passed the Party Funding Law in July 2014 and reduced the portion of the annual budget allocated to political party financing to 1%. Civil society organizations have valid criticisms that the law does not reach the level sufficient to reduce the burden on the public budget, including allocation of $54,493 per seat per month to each party and the way the seats were allocated after the last two elections. The Movement for Change (Gouran) says it had to agree to these changes to get the law's support from the Patriotic Union of Kurdistan. The movement promised that it would be ready to agree with other parties after six months to reduce the amount allocated to each seat by half. The law will be implemented as soon as the current economic crisis ends. Despite these valid criticisms, the endorsement of the law is an important and positive development. Politically, the law regulates party financing through legislation. This will put an end to the KDP and the PUK's misuse of part of the public budget and ensure equality and fairness between the parties to some extent by allocating funds based on the number of seats.

Economically, this means that the Treasury will save $840 million annually, which is equivalent to approximately one month's salary for all employees. There is no guarantee that the KDP and the Patriotic Union of Kurdistan, or the other dominant parties in the future, will not attempt to change the law to serve their interests. However, this will not be easy because the application of the law will set a legal precedent and create a new dynamic that will not be easy to reverse. The public's growing demands that citizenship rights be respected are pushing the Patriotic Union of Kurdistan and the Kurdistan Democratic Party (KDP) to acknowledge the need for other gradual and modest reforms and to promise to implement them. In his inauguration speech in Parliament as Prime Minister in the eighth government on June 5, 2014, Nechirvan Barzani said: "Citizenship will become the principle and value, and the main measure of government activities ... The eighth ministry will create the appropriate environment to ensure that Parliament can monitor government activities appropriately as it should. The eighth's ministry shall review and organize the pension and salary system so that it benefits people in a fair way". Time will reveal to us to which extent these promises are committed to and how many will be fulfilled. However, mounting public pressure and the economic crisis affecting the region seem to be exerting some influence. In 2015, the Ministry of Finance and Economy, led by the Change Movement

(Guran), began a gradual reform of illegal salaries and pensions. The Ministry gave persons associated with the Patriotic Union of Kurdistan and the Kurdistan Democratic Party (KDP) who receive two salaries a period of two months to announce their source of income, and then they must choose one salary and give up the other. And if they do not comply, they will have to pay back all of the money they got. Parliamentary blocs are also discussing proposals to address the issue of people who receive salaries but do not work. Civil society groups and the former opposition have long called for the creation of an independent higher election body, and there appears to be progress on that front as well. Parliament approved the law establishing a new body on July 23, 2014, and it was approved by President Masoud Barzani one month later. The former Iraqi commission was monopolized by the KDP and the Patriotic Union of Kurdistan, and critics frequently complained of election fraud and intimidation. Under the new law, the members of the nine board of directors - from the five major political parties in the region - are elected by an absolute majority in parliament, and they are accountable to parliament. Civil society activists say that the new body is not independent but rather partisan and that its members will not be independent professionals. In addition, Parliament published an advertisement to fill the nine vacancies that attracted 200 applications. Ultimately, the five major blocs in parliament, including the former opposition, chose party candidates. In the years 2015 and 2017, when presidential and parliamentary elections are expected to be held respectively, it will be clear to what extent this law and the new body will succeed in reducing or eliminating the phenomenon of election fraud and manipulation. While the prime minister promised in his inauguration speech that his government would guarantee transparency and accountability, he subsequently made a decision that showed the old habits do not disappear easily. Nechirvan Barzani allocated $30,000 to each new minister from outside Erbil to spend on re-furnishing their places of residence in the capital. That decision angered public opinion, especially at a time when the region was going through an economic crisis and waging war against the Islamic State. As a result, all ministers from the previous opposition groups, the Change Movement (Gouran), the Kurdistan Islamic Union and the Islamic Group in Kurdistan refused to allocate this amount, prompting the PUK ministers to do the same. In addition, one of the biggest challenges facing the former opposition, which is now part of the government, is to avoid its co-optation due to corrupt practices in the system. The majority of members of the Kurdish parliament, including the majority of the former opposition, asked the Presidency of Parliament (which consists of the president, the vice president, and the secretary) to buy them cars that would enable them to make field visits. It has been reported that Parliament will buy 111 cars, at a total cost of about $6 million. The Secretary of Parliament said that these cars would be the property of Parliament. In another incident, the appointment of two officials from the Change Movement (Gouran), one of whom was said to not hold the necessary university degrees to assume the position of Assistant Minister of Finance and Economy, led to a wave of criticism about favouritism. However, in an indication of the increasing importance of activity, public opinion, and the demands of the supporters of the Change Movement (Gouran), public pressure led to the resignation of the official who did not have the required university degree. For its part, the independent media in Kurdistan have become more assertive and effective in following up on human rights violations and corruption cases. In some cases, women's rights organizations have succeeded in stirring up anger over the increase in violence against women. The constant pressure from families of victims of the "Anfal" genocide, in which forces loyal to Saddam Hussein killed thousands of Kurdish civilians in the late 1980s, prompted the Kurdistan Regional Government to arrest a Kurdish collaborator who had been pardoned by the KDP and the Patriotic Union of Kurdistan. The Iraqi authorities issued arrest warrants for these collaborators, but the KDP and the Patriotic Union of Kurdistan refused to arrest them. These cases demonstrate to activists the importance of the ongoing demand to address impunity and engage public opinion on various issues. The parliamentary elections held on September 21, 2013, reshaped the political map in the Kurdistan region. The KDP and the Patriotic Union of Kurdistan participated separately in the elections. The Patriotic Union of Kurdistan was the biggest loser, and it was replaced by the Change Movement (Gouran) as the second-largest party. It took the Kurdistan Regional Government approximately eight months to form the new government. Parliament wanted to keep its sessions open until a new government was formed. Civil society actors have filed a complaint with the Administrative Court in Erbil against the Deputy Speaker of Parliament, calling for an end to the open session in Parliament and warning that if the Erbil Court does not rule on the case, they will file a complaint with the Federal Court in Baghdad. This would have been a source of great embarrassment for the judiciary and the Kurdish authorities. Ultimately, civil society actors won the case. At the beginning of 2014, Shwan Saber, a judge and investigator with the Regional Judicial Council, used his Facebook page to criticize the Supreme Judicial Council for its lack of impartiality and to say that courts in Kurdistan are not independent. After a complaint filed by the Council, the court in Erbil ruled that he should be arrested. However, Saber was released on bail, on March 6, 2014, after intense pressure from lawyers and activists. Some activities receive less media attention, but nonetheless, they set interesting precedents for protest groups. One-person demonstrations and sit-ins are new forms of activism and a sign of the increasing politicization of society. However, this does not mean that mass protests are becoming less common, as activists and individual citizens continue to take to the streets to express their criticism of the regime. With regard to reforming the oil sector, and after intense pressure from activists, the media, and the former opposition, in 2015, Parliament passed a law allowing the establishment of a sovereign fund for oil and gas revenues under its supervision. The aim of this law was to limit the power of party conglomerates in this sector by institutionalizing revenue management and ensuring that it will be used to serve current and future generations. Most of these cumulative changes may not have immediate impacts on the main foundations of the sultan's system. Nevertheless, it shows the determination of civil and political actors to challenge the system and achieve gradual reforms. Therefore, in this regard, the interaction between citizenship and the sultanate should be viewed as an ongoing struggle. The politicized society was able to prevent the semi-authoritarian regime from sliding into absolute despotism. It maintained a margin of freedom, increased the awareness of society, and gradually expanded civil spaces. However, the limited nature of these changes is a product of the restrictive environment in which Kurdistan has become more politicized.

Complex Environment: It seems that the former opposition and the majority of activists and intellectuals are all in agreement on the need to reform the system, not to overthrow it through the revolution. This obstacle can be explained by the internal and external framework in which these forces operate. Amidst the Middle East plagued by sectarian violence, religious extremism represented by the Islamic State and other extremist groups, and the collapse of state institutions, the issue of gradual reforms and nonviolence are more persuasive than revolutionary ruptures. However, the population has lost patience with the PUK, the KDP, and the former opposition. They are angered by the rampant corruption at the highest levels, conscious of their rights, high hopes, and demanding swift and structural changes. This is partly due to the development and empowerment of society, and in the other part to the successful attempt by the Change Movement (Gouran) to mobilize voters and the opposition from 2009 to 2013. In addition, the intelligence and security services, the police and the peshmerga remain partisan and loyal to the KDP and the PUK. Kurdistan, as the suppression of the two-month demonstrations in 2011 demonstrated, is ready to use military force against civilian opposition. The war against the Islamic State has once again highlighted the partisan nature of these forces. Most of the Peshmerga forces belong to Units 70 and 80, which are commanded by military leaders from the Patriotic Union of Kurdistan and the Kurdistan Democratic Party and are subject to their command and control, not to the Ministry of Peshmerga Affairs in the Kurdistan Regional Government. This fragmented and weakened the fight against the Islamic State. At the same time, this situation highlighted the urgent need to place all forces under the command of the Ministry of Peshmerga Affairs. At the beginning of 2015, President Masoud Barzani issued his orders to place Units 70 and 80 under the leadership of the ministry, which is managed by the Change Movement (Gouran), but this decision has not yet been implemented. A small but encouraging sign of reform is that all members of the Peshmerga units now get their salaries from the ministry, not from the KDP or the Patriotic Union of Kurdistan. In addition, the ministry has floated the idea of creating new units composed of young men recruited into military service that would be accountable to the ministry and not to the KDP or the Patriotic Union of Kurdistan. At present, the KDP does not seem to be against these ideas. But it is not clear yet whether the two parties will give the Change Movement (Gouran) more power and room to carry out a structural reform process for the Ministry of Peshmerga and turn it into a non-partisan national force. The Uncertainty about the final status of the Kurdistan region in Iraq, including what its borders will be and whether it will be independent or remain part of federal Iraq, impedes the development of a politicized society to a further extent. The KDP and the Patriotic Union of Kurdistan are taking advantage of this issue to divert attention from pressing social and political problems. For example, in the current debate about the independence of Kurdistan, the KDP posits itself and Barzani, through the media, statements and political activities, as the only two parties seeking independence, portraying their critics as traitors. But despite this strategy of distraction, social protests against delayed salary payments, the fuel and electricity crisis, human rights violations, and corruption continued, showing that the PUK and the KDP may be able to divert attention from real policy issues for some time, but the discontent Social and political will not fade away. Turkey and Iran, the two main regional powers, have great influence over the political and economic affairs of the Kurdistan Region Government, and both have strategic interests in preserving the political status quo in Kurdistan. Turkey and the AKP, in particular, are strategic partners of the KDP. Turkish companies are the largest investors in the region, as Kurdish oil exports depend on Turkey. Turkish President Rejab Tayyib Erdogan has described Masoud Barzani as the leader of all Kurds, not only in Iraq but also in Turkey, Iran, and Syria. The Kurdistan Democratic Party as the model Kurdish party; And the Kurdistan Regional Government as the economic model that all Kurds should follow. Iran is a strategic partner for the Patriotic Union of Kurdistan (PUK), especially the Talabani faction. This partnership is so important that Iran is said to have helped prevent a historic defeat for the Patriotic Union of Kurdistan in the Iraqi elections in April 2014. In the regional sectarian conflicts in Syria and Iraq, the KDP and the PUK are part of two contradictory axes: The KDP is part of the Jordan, Qatar, Saudi Arabia, and Turkey axis, while the Patriotic Union of Kurdistan is part of the Iran axis. Both parties have collaborated extensively with these regional (and international) powers on political, economic, and intelligence issues and are using these external strategic partnerships to strengthen the internal sultanic order. The shape of the Change Movement (Gouran) and other former opposition parties in the future will also help determine the extent of Kurdistan's politicization. This will depend on the amount of power and space these parties will gain from the KDP and the Patriotic Union of Kurdistan to initiate reforms and on their determination and ability to offer an alternative model of politics and politicians, one that is not corrupt and able to resist attempts to co-opt it by the regime. The adoption of party finance laws, the High Elections Commission, the Ministry of Peshmerga Affairs, salaries, and pension systems are small but positive steps. In addition, reforming the oil sector will be a major test for the former opposition. However, it will take time for these reforms to yield results and for their effects to be measured. Meanwhile, the people of the region are alarmed and want to see rapid structural changes. The former opposition, especially the Change Movement (Gouran), is also facing what might be called the dilemma of mobilization and governance. When they were in opposition, these groups succeeded in mobilizing sections of the population against the sultan's regime. But when I became in government, I faced the reality of translating electoral promises into implementable policies and implementing successful reforms. The battle against ISIS makes the task of initiating reforms more complicated because implementing structural changes and measuring their impact requires a stable social and political environment. The battle against the Islamic State has provided the PUK and the KDP with the excuse that they cannot implement reforms due to the need to focus on combating the terrorist threat. On Mountain of Sinjar, where the KDP's peshmerga withdrew without firing a single shot on August 3, 2014, the Yazidis left to their fate were outraged that the party had failed to protect them. Even some Yezidis said that they were no longer Kurds. It is therefore impossible to predict how this anger will affect the outcome of the upcoming elections and whether this will lead to a decline in support for the KDP. The withdrawal from the

Mountain of Sinjar and other areas had an unintended but positive effect. It emphasized the structural weakness of party military units in Kurdistan and accelerated the need to create a national military force. In its fight against the Islamic State, the Kurdistan Regional Government is getting military and political support from Western countries, Iran, and Turkey. However, the question that dominates the debate in the region is: Will the Islamic State be defeated, and when, and is there any guarantee that the KDP and the Patriotic Union of Kurdistan will not use these weapons against each other as well as against the political opposition and civic actors [https: //carnegie-mec.org].

The Absence of National Identity and Its Destructive Effects

I do not overlook what this theory brought about from a very national, sensitive, and necessary issue for every Iraqi, which is the betrayal of many Iraqis and their treason of the homeland that has lasted for more than half a century from several parties, military, sectarian and tribal components. Is it reasonable that the Iraqis do not have a sense of patriotism? Why do the Iraqi parties, sects and tribes seek empowerment from the foreigner in their rule of their country when they are among their Iraqi people? Who is responsible for this shameful and disgraceful characteristic? Especially since it is the main source of instability in the country. Therefore, we present it at the end of the theoretical construction because it is the core of the problems that the Iraqis suffered from and contributed to the squandering of its wealth, plundering it and donating it to Iran, America and Britain, while the Iraqi society did not benefit from it in building and progress, the effects are:-

1. Transfer of national loyalty to the seat of the ruler.
2. Empowerment by foreign powers which are greedy for Iraq's wealth.
3. Betrayal of the homeland in order to change the political system.
4. The absence of conscious collective base.

Each individual has his own and public affiliations that represent his extended roots in the social soil, such as belonging to his childbearing family, to his nationality in which he grew up through his family, to his religion that he acquired from his parents and his community, and to his city or village, where he has memories that impressed in his memory. And he has another affiliation, which is a general and great that gives him his national document and history, so these affiliations are among the constants of loyalty to his nation that he cannot change or replace, such as his loyalty to his family, religion, and nationality. However, there are circumstances, incubators, and motives that push him to switch his loyalty from his homeland to another country so that he becomes an agent to a political system other than his country's one and start servicing it and receives its instructions to spy on his society for the benefit of the other system he devoted his loyalty to. Simply, it means he is a traitor to his original country in which he was born, raised, and educated in order to take over in his country. These loyalties are linked to the identity of citizenship. If such loyalties are embraced with the loyalty nature that includes love, sincerity, loyalty, and identification with it, then his national identity would be integral, deep and devoted to his family, religion, nationality and country, and vice versa. However, there are factors such as poverty, unemployment, national, religious, sectarian, and partisan fanaticism that are practised against him makes his loyalty to his homeland gradually vanished, especially if it is practised by a tyrannical, fanatic, and unjust ruler in his dealings with social components. Yes, that is right because it contradicts his national loyalty as he feels he is excluded, marginalized, or excluded from the will, deprived of freedom of thought, and not participating in the process of local and national decision-making. It is therefore classified as a national betrayal as it is against the regime of the ruler of his country, while the main cause of such betrayal is the ruler of the country who used the security services to protect him instead of protecting the homeland and consolidating its authority, thus spreading terror and social phobia on members of society and exploiting his power for the rich at the expense of the country's wealth, thus impoverishing society without providing basic services in the infrastructure and middle.

It is ludicrous and ridiculous that this despotic tyrant president who seized power by rape rather than by-election was also reinforced by external foreign powers in his acquisition of the power. These foreign powers were greedy and aiming at confiscating the wealth of their country plus obtaining materialistic and political gains. That what was found in the Iraqi society during the monarchy rule, which was supported by Britain, while Qasim, Saadi, and Saddam's rule were reinforced by America, and finally the Da'wa Party which has the full support of Iran. All of them were reinforced and empowered by greedy foreign powers without whom they would never become rulers of Iraq. This situation has prevailed in Iraq for more than seventy years and until now. So, it can be said that the marginalized individuals, political parties, religious sects, and ethnic minorities of the society resort to foreign powers seeking support to get rid of their tyrannical ruler, who is also supported by major foreign powers to consolidate his power and rule. Therefore, the ruler of the country is also an agent traitorous, and at the same time, he pushes many Individuals, parties and sects to fall into the arms of foreign powers to defend themselves. The betrayal of the ruler and his stand with foreign powers, in addition to his tyranny over his people, produce agents and traitors in order to topple him. Thus, the country, the ruler and the community are all under the strength of the foreigner's bullying and blackmailing, so that the agents' loyalties to the foreigner spread, and the betrayal becomes a phenomenon that does not constitute a national problem. Moreover, such betrayal is converted into means of greed, influence, and revenge, so that the country becomes an arena for competition between the ruler, political parties, sectarian and national groups, and foreign powers (America, Britain, and neighbouring countries) in order to win power by rape rather than through elections. This competition is not without bloody armed conflicts between contenders for power. Unfortunately, all this caused the vanish of national identity among the members of society, and the way was opened to all traitors to seek help and reinforcement from foreigners in order to usurp and seize power. This is what has happened in Iraq, Libya, Syria, Yemen, Lebanon, Yemen, Sudan, and Tunisia. When military and political coups take place, they for sure lead to the disruption of the social fabric and civil strife within society because such coups are coupled with a fanaticism that results in an exacerbated partisan, sectarian, and nationalist in the society. That is why the Arab society, especially in Iraq, Syria, Lebanon, Libya, Yemen, Sudan, Egypt, and Tunisia, is suffering at the present time from situations that can be described as they are the crisis that the Arab community pays the price for. However, the generation of young people who are conscious and politically enlightened in light of the information revolution, technologies and satellite channels that expose the hidden among these rulers and foreign powers that targeting the wealth of their country rose up and revolted against them, but these rulers are still dependent on foreign powers, not because they are in love with these rulers, but rather to subjugate them and steal the wealth of their countries and harness them to their will which converted the society to retarded, crushed and shredded society. Therefore, the loss of patriotism of the members of the Arab community was caused by its rulers who have assigned loyalty to them instead of to the homeland and used the security services to terrorize the people instead of protecting them. Accordingly, the citizenship and its homeland identity have been lost, and such a loss was translated into a lack of national responsibility, lack of sincerity in work, and the practice of financial, political, moral, and religious corruption has widely spread because the objective of these (national) rulers was to defend their rule and to assign the loyalty to themselves rather than to defend and being loyal to the homeland. It is a national crisis of heavyweights that needs a massive and sweeping revolution on them so that the scenario is not repeated again in the coming decades and with the emerging Arab generations.

It goes without saying that national loyalty and betrayal to the homeland are two opposing, contradictory, and antagonistic concepts, but they exist in a society whose political and social system does not exercise justice in its politics and its dealings with the components of society. Since the society consists of several nationalities, religions, sects, and parties, achieving social justice with them is a necessary need for stability and solidarity in society. As for its injustice, betrayal appears in the lack of identification and symmetry with the stability and level of social life, then the state of disloyalty emerges and goes to the state of betrayal, which is a cause and a step that the enemy takes to the homeland and to the social fabric. No harm in clarifying the betrayal as breaking trust, disloyalty, and breaching loyalty, which is acquired, not inherited. The loyalty to the country and sincerity in work tend to avenge the ruling regime's policy and the strife that has been intolerant against it. Treachery precedes agency for the foreigner, and loyalty, which is the opposite of treason and betrayal, means identification and conformity to ethical standards and rules on which the individual was brought up in his family, his school, his religion, and his party. Therefore, the case of betrayal to a foreigner clearly shows among the groups, fanatic against them and their legitimate rights, which pushes them to be empowered by the enemy who is greedy in the wealth of their country. That led to the emergence of many political movements against the dictatorships, which were empowered by foreign powers eager to plunder their country's goods. It is an anomaly and a pathological condition that Arab societies have lived through since the middle of the last century until now, which is that all their rulers of various affiliations have usurped the power of government by force and with the help of external foreign powers (America, Britain, France, Iran, and Israel), which made this situation simulated and imitated. It seeks the help of foreign powers to support them in order to change a regime of government that is also empowered by a foreigner, so coups and conspiracies take place in Arab countries. With the repetition of this anomaly, betrayal by rulers, parties, sects, and nationalities has become unashamed and does not bring them shame, disgrace, and betrayal in its old sense, but rather a necessary need to change the regime. All of this is due to the absence of the spirit of citizenship among the Arab, which the ruler has transformed into his identity, considering himself a symbol of the homeland, and he does not deal with his people as citizens, but as slaves and a herd of sheep, which makes them fall into the bosom of a foreigner seeking empowerment. But if there was a patriotic loyalty inculcated by the family and school curricula that the homeland is belonging to the land and not to the leader, sincerity to work and to serve people, not to serve the ruler, not to be intolerant and prejudiced in dealing with members of society, and to assume institutional responsibility as a national duty not as a presidential duty and not to disturb the security system, not for fear of repressive systems, but in order to protect people's security and respect the opposing opinion, in appreciation of his thinking. This is a sense of patriot loyalty, which is impermeable to the existence of treachery among individuals, and to hold the tyrant ruler accountable to a foreigner and isolate him because he does not have national loyalty. Finally, we say that the crisis of the Arab community that has befallen it for more than three-quarters of a century upon which the national identity has been lost though it was not one of its characteristics, rather obliterated by the tyrannical ruler who made himself a symbol of the country and was tied with a foreigner and practised favouritism, patronage and intolerance against his opponents and the use of security services to defend it and not to establish security for citizens. For all of this, the Iraqi and the Arab are suffering from being without a national identity. It was stolen from him for decades, but the time has come to demand it, which will make him pay dearly for it from his life and deprive him of his legitimate rights.

Based on the above, and in order to scrutinize the foregoing, let present the Iraqi example, where the Iraqi Communist Party during the rule of Qasim was an agent of the Soviet Union (formerly), and the Baath Party was an agent of the American administration and the Shiite Da'wa Party was an agent of the Guardian of Jurist in Iran, as well as the Iraqi Hezbollah, while Al-Islami party is an agent of Turkey, Qatar, Saudi Arabia, and the Kurdistan Democratic Party is an agent of America and Israel, and the agency of the Muslim Brotherhood Party in Egypt and Kuwait to America. It is ludicrous that all of these parties claim to be patriotic, but in reality, they did not serve Iraq and the Iraqis. Why is this agency for foreign powers? The answer is caused by the individual agent rule of foreign powers as well and by the fanatical dictatorial rule of one social group. All of them did not possess the national identity because it was not brought upon it. This is a punishable catastrophe for the Iraqi society, which revealed its absence, pushing some citizens to compete for the acquisition of power not to serve the citizens or to build a nation or to assume responsibility for community service. Therefore, the agency became desirable and wanted instead of loyalty to the homeland, and betrayal became one requirement for authoritarian rule. Corruption spread in all its political, economic, administrative, judicial, and educational forms, which made Iraq and the Iraqis victims of these. As for the solution and treatment to this critical problem, it is the application of positive law, sincerity in work, non-monopoly of power, reduced factional fanaticism, respect for other opinions, and political freedom for citizens. This is what is missing in the content of the national identity in Iraq. It is right to say that when the national identity is lost among the citizens, the tendency of disloyalty to the country emerges and is replaced by the tendency of loyalty to the foreigner and betrayal of the homeland. Such tendency is coupled with the state of nonadopting of orthodox moral standards, which spreads without shyness or shame. The situation is aggravated especially when the symbols of the authority who are the basis of governance are deprived of this identity; hence others are encouraged to imitate them and simulate their violence of moral and national controls. Also, the spread of the phenomenon of political and moral corruption without considering it a social problem, but rather an acceptable and welcome context. Therefore, the advocate of objectivity, impartiality, community service and the country become accused and angry at the guardians and be hostile to the society and the ruling system. The concept of security will not then be used to serve the security of society, but to terrorize, suppress, imprison, and torture it in the name of security, which is in fact the security of the ruler, his symbols, and his eminence, not the general public, and this is what has been prevalent in Iraqi society for decades. In other words, it is the preservation of the ruler's security and his rule rather than the security of the people. Injustice, oppression, and imprisonment of individual and political freedoms prevail due to ignorance in the application of justice, transparency, and integrity. This is the biggest reason for the backwardness of the society. The absence of national loyalty, however, removes societal security, and the society becomes fragmented and differentiated between groups. In this context, the one who is loyal to the ruler, whether by fear, falsely, or hypocrisy, is considered a good citizen, while who is not loyal to the ruler is considered hostile to the homeland and society. This means that misconceptions prevail over social life to become concepts and standards of official life and not customary, and this distorts the standards and values of social culture adopted by society. But will these misconceptions be perpetuated forever? The answer is no because it does not serve the common people but rather some of them. In light of the foregoing, is that the absence of national identity among Iraqis since the middle of the last century until now has made them struggle over the acquisition of power and its authority. It has made Iraq a theatre and arena for foreign powers competing for its wealth. And the loyalty of the rulers is transformed to gain authority rather than benefiting the country. Moreover, they become active agents to the foreigner to remain in power, while the betrayal by the parties which are against the Iraqi ruler became a weapon to change him. However, on 1st Oct 2019, the conscious youth of Iraq rose up demanding the national identity and loyalty to the homeland instead of loyalty to the political party, religious sect, national fanaticism, accountability and punishment of agents and traitors. This is a new awakening of a generation that Iraq has not seen in its modern history.

The effects of the national identity absence in Iraq have resulted in the following:

1.   A bloody struggle between the people of the same country, between Sunnis and Shiites, both of the same religion, the Communists with the Baathists, and both are Iraqis, the Shiite Da'wa Party, and the Sunni Islamic Party, both of whom are Muslims.

2.   The formation of armed militias infiltrating the security services, killing citizens who oppose them.

3.   The existence of secret prisons for opponents of the ruling party, both Iraqis, and the displacement of Iraqis from their country.

4.   Iraqis resort to foreign countries while they are Iraqis. Bombings are planned in popular areas, and they are Iraqis.

5.   Formation of party armies against the parties opposing the government (the Popular Resistance, the National Guard, the People's Army, the Popular Mobilization Forces).

6.   The spread of bribery, embezzlement, forgery, and exploitation of government positions.

7.   Smuggling of oil, hard currency, heritage relics, and the Iraqi treasury.

8.   Torture of prisoners

9.   The politicization of religion.

10.   The politicization of the military and security institutions whose function is to defend the homeland and protect the citizen.

11.   The high rate of illiteracy.

12.   Destruction and burning of government buildings.

13.   Fight against free thought. All these practices are caused by the loss of national feeling among Iraqis and the prevalence of partisan, sectarian, tribal, and regional fanaticism. Therefore, the Iraqis have become a unified human gathering, not a unified

community, with a long-standing social culture that mixes Iraqis with the unity of land, history, religion, values, and inherited norms.

Theoretical Proposal

It is noticed that most of the members of the agent parties before they were brought to Iraq and installed as rulers were not practising theft, crime, intimidation, fraud or fraud in European countries and Iran. They were refugees and immigrants who did not work and did not have official positions in the presence of a system and laws in place and peoples respecting order and discipline legal. But when they became one of the holders of the highest positions, representing the government, and under their responsibilities, the trust of its administration and preservation of its properties, and no one held them accountable, even the people who subjected them by force, fire, iron, imprisonment, and torture, they appeared to be unattended, neither by authority nor by a people, so they acted freely without being restricted by law, customary or religious controls. They took advantage of the responsibilities of their positions and exaggerated their guardianship, responsibilities, and official banks, stealing public money and smuggling it abroad, taking commissions on every deal, falsifying government projects, and not implementing them. They practised fraud, forgery, smuggling, theft and abuse of responsibility and the position that no one holds accountable to them, neither courts nor parliament, except for non-governmental media outlets. So, they levied the laws in their favour and donated billions of dollars to their Iranian masters because they took care of them during their asylum in Iran. This is what made us say or reach a logical formula according to which when a person is under the penalty of the law, he becomes upright, honest, abides by the law as long as he does not occupy a high and leadership position or has the reins of affairs, but just a simple employee or beneficiary of social security. But when he occupies a high and leadership position and holds the reins of affairs in his hands, his behaviour becomes criminal's behaviour and absurdist by monopolizing power and circumventing the laws and tampering with the capabilities of people without national, human, or religious feelings. They were amazed by power and money because they lacked prestige, influence, and sincere respect, meaning that they lacked any customary controls in their social conscience, and they did not understand the responsibilities of the higher and leadership positions but remained at the bottom of the social pyramid. When they became rulers, however, they removed the law and totally ignored it, so they freely disposed of the money and the property of the people and stole billions. In general, when the clerics of the agent parties lived in civilized societies, they did not practise corruption, and their behaviour was full of integrity, but when they became responsible, they returned back to their past before living in exile. The people and the government did not reform or rebuild anything but supported all their corruption with the militias of their parties, which were hostile to everyone who was not subject to them. They made the ministries their palaces and state property as a war spoil. They are traitors with a distinction, and It had not happened before that Iraq is ruled by anyone similar to them. They bankrupted the rich Iraq and making his sons live under the poverty line, depriving the jobs of the educated and university youth of Iraq. They festered intellectuals, scholars and professionals, and displaced Iraqis, thus caused gaps in its population pyramid. They did not serve their sects, but abused them, made their parties a means of financial enrichment, fighting Iraqis, and carried out social movements and youth uprisings, and planted corruption in all state institutions. They became political tyrants, financial tycoons, and sectarian merchants.

Theoretical Statement

1. Trading in religion is a game brought about by the American occupier and fed by the Persian power.

2. Iran cannot see Iraq as a strong country, and the Iraqis enjoy their wealth because of their hostility to the national and religious authenticity that Iraqi society enjoys.

3. External conflict does not necessarily lead to permanent internal solidarity of the conflicting group.

4. Sectarian (Shiite and Sunni) and tribal (Kurdish) parties were not intermediaries between the people and the government.

5. Sectarian and tribal parties have armed militias that use them against all of the Iraqi people who oppose them. This means that they are like an armed gang wrapped in a shining party cover.

6. The announcement by these parties of their agency to the foreigner in a blatant manner without shame means it is not pure Iraqi patriotism.

7. These parties did not represent mass movements that aimed to rebuild and build Iraq but rather to steal it and sabotage its structural patterns.

8. These parties have their deep state in every ministry to implement their private interests, not the public ones.

9. Feeding sentimental feelings by the Shiite clergy, not the rational Shiite thought.

10. The tyranny of the ruler over his people through his empowerment by the foreigner produces agents for the foreigner and betrayed the homeland and vice versa.

11. The citizen does not feel patriotic if the ruler does not hold him the national responsibility.

12. Ethnic, religious, and party fanaticism results in betrayal against the fanatic.

13. When the national identity is lost among the citizens, the loyalty to the homeland vanishes and is replaced by a loyalty to the foreigner and betrayal of the homeland and vice versa.

14. Usurpers rulers tend to foreigners to reinforce their presidency.

15. The tyrannical ruler indirectly pushes marginalized groups into the arms of foreign agencies to get rid of him.

16. The loss of the Iraqi national identity is caused by the uniqueness and tyranny of their rulers, who made the loyalty to their rule instead of loyalty to Iraq.

17. The absence of the Iraqi national identity has led to the spread of political, financial, and administrative corruption among Iraqis.

18. Repeated political coup in Iraq is attributed to the absence of national identity and its substitution by the loyalty to the foreigner.

19. Whoever becomes an agent to the foreigner sacrifices his riding on a permanent basis.

Theory Axioms

The agent parties (strengthened by the foreigner) served and carried out the interests and ambitions inside Iraq for the interest of those who strengthened them. They were hostile to the national unity and robbed its wealth and donated it to the foreigner without hesitation and shame. They corrupted the policies of institutions in all parts of the state (internal, external, financial, security, military, religious, educational and health) and deprived Iraqis of their legitimate rights and agricultural and fishery wealth and froze industries. It was betrayal par excellence. The surprising thing about these agent ruling parties is that they condemned the previous government for its tyranny and oppression during its rule of Iraq, but their performance was much worse than what they condemned. They were more arbitrary, tyrannical, and oppressing than it. Knowing that the previous regime did not steal or plunder the wealth of Iraq, but these agent parties did so. It simply means that the tyranny of the rulers of Iraq is rotating with every ruler who came through foreigner strengthening. And it seems that such a strengthening generates another strengthening to remove the current ruler and so on. The agent ruling parties have not learned from the end of the tyranny of previous governments, as if they were copying their policies, but in a larger, wider, and ugliest fashion, the Iraqis have become victims of the despotism and

211

tyranny of the rulers throughout the ages on a continuous basis. It can be said the despotism in power among the rulers of Iraq is rotated from one ruler to another, as if they were one face, with the agent ruling parties superior to the former rulers by plundering, stealing, terrorizing, and killing free citizens and undermining the unified national identity of the Iraqis. We should point out that not all Shiites, Sunnis and Kurds are agents, as there is Iraqi youth from these components which have become enlightened and aware of the arbitrariness and corruption of their rulers. Mass communications and immediate social media technologies helped the conscious youth to rise, uprising and revolt against the agent parties in peaceful protests of two million people, particularly in the western region, south, central, and north of Iraq. The slogans that were raised in these protests were against corruption and thefts, the lack of participation in decision-making and the denial of work in official institutions. They are the first of the conscious and enlightened generation that will lead Iraq away from the style of the strengthening by the foreigner (being agent). They are appraising and glorifying the national affiliation and purifying their community from the agents imposed on them by the foreign strengthening of the agent parties.

Among the fruits of the theory case are the following:

1.   The tails raped the three authorities (political, financial, sectarian, and tribal).

2. The tails fought against the Iraqi national unity by replacing sectarian and tribal loyalty with national loyalty and loyalty.

3. The tails seized power and squandered the wealth of the country.

4. The tails displaced Iraq's competencies and assassinated its security and military leaders.

5. The tails imposed civil, intellectual, and scientific backwardness in Iraq through their exaggeration in practising sectarian rituals dating back centuries and not pushing it towards looking to the future.

6. The tails afflicted the Iraqis with multiple and varied psychological and social diseases (drug addiction, suicide, depression, behavioural deviations, non-normality substituting normality, violence, and social phobia).

Generalisations of the Theory

1. The exploitation of religion by politicians leads to distortions of religion due to their lack of awareness of its humanity and tolerance, as both are incompatible in their goals and principles because religion is for everyone and politics is for the fraudulent, vulnerable, and circumstantial opportunism.

2. Iraq will only be governed by its enlightened and aware sons who believe in the cultural and religious diversity and not by the unbelievers, the foreign agents and the thieves of the era.

3. Tribal control provokes inter-tribal conflict, monopolizing power and plundering public money.

4. When the law is applied and adhered to by the citizens, fraudulent practices, thefts, smuggling, sabotage, and agency for foreigners decrease.

5. Corruption is spread in all its forms when public groups imitate and simulate the special groups sitting on top of authority.

6. The tyrannical ruler who seeks to strengthen his authority confiscation by a foreigner makes the citizen refuse his homeland and vice versa.

7. All members of the agent parties obtained a vertical social compete raised from below the level of

poverty to above the level of poverty, but in spite of that, this social did not give them a sincere social consideration or real social influence and did not make them community leaders, reformers, thinkers, or planners, but they remained as denies who are stigmatized with tails, thieves, and the revengers from every patriot who demands his national rights. They do not have a cultural, scientific, or religious competency, but rather they have tricks of fraud, evasion, foxy manoeuvring, and treachery as a chameleon.

8. They have no roots in the national or religious soil, but they appear in putrid water swamps. They only grow in turbulent and polluted atmospheres. Therefore, they have no future in genuine Iraq in its land and religion.

Laws of Theory

1. When the postural controls are absent, the corruption of the senior officials outcrops before the younger ones.

2. When customary controls are absent, the normative value in people's lives disappears and is replaced by the non-normative value, which becomes dominant in society.

3. The national ruler does not emerge except through his national milieu and not from the foreign milieu.

4. Exercising three powers (political, financial, and sectarian) at the same time and with one hand, leading to structural disorder and an imbalance in thinking, appreciation and dealing with the other.

5. An oppressive despotic ruler who is strengthened by a foreigner is a source of national opposition and vice versa.

6. Agency precedes betrayal, and both are the same and opposes the national affiliation.

7. The fate of recruits for the foreign agency is linked to the recruits' support for them, and when this connection finishes, they are expelled from the society that they conspired against and profane its principles and religion, and when the recruits

abandon them, they become rejected and despised by public opinion.

8. The recruiter for the agency for a foreigner does not have a national identity but rather holds the identity of a mercenary hired for a foreigner.

9. The exploitation of the religious community for the benefit of the political ruling system does not last because of the difference in their starting points and goals (the first is spiritual and sacred, the second is subjective and circumstantial interest).

10. The political quota is the source of fundamental institutional corruption in the country.

Theoretical Prediction

Social theory often makes a prediction of upcoming events in light of what you read and analyse. And since our theory is about contemporary society, which possesses the structural and systemic pillars that are extended in the depths of history, but the society remains constant in its growth and movement. Sometimes slowing down and in other times accelerating in its movement, but not vanishing or disappearing, but rather is subject to evolving change, not changing. Meaning, the social culture, nationalities, races and sects of the Iraqi society will remain regardless of what happened to it from foreign invasion, foreign occupation, theft of its wealth, the destruction of its factories and farms, and the corruption of its morals in drugs and deviations. However, such viral diseases cannot continue and will not settle in the Iraqi society body because it has a natural immune system that rejects and spells out these viruses. It is directed like the rest of the waves that ravage societies. It comes and goes and remains steadfast to gain immunity from these emerging diseases and to come out healthy and purify his body from these boils and ulcers that cannot eat away the body of the society as it has a strong structure. The hindrance of the Iraqi society movement by the invader, the occupier and the avenger is not permanent. It is for a limited period of time, after which it purifies its body from these strange ills and builds itself with elements that represent its age, not the age of its ancestors. Society will acquire a new spirit and mentality with new young elements that build, not destroy. As for the generation that has ruined and destroyed society, its strength will be weakened and will disappear with time. It will not then be able to face the requirements of the age because of its sterility in thinking and exposing its corruption, fraud, and intolerance. Political change in Iraq, therefore, seems to be inevitably coming at the hands of the poor, the unemployed, those with national consciousness, and those who were tricked by the sectarian hoax, and not at the hands of political foundlings. This is very much expected because the country's economy has deteriorated and unemployment has worsened among professionals and academics, and the public money has been stolen in public and in secrecy at the hands of the agents and the feudal lords of power. No matter how hard they cling to their agents, militias, and fanatical factional parties, the will of the downtrodden will get over those who are surrounded by the no-man money. Likewise, change is coming after the Iranian regime falls. These agent parties will flee out of Iraq with militias because their presence depends on the existence of the mullahs' regime in Iran.

Social and Preventive Treatments for This Problem

The remedies for this social disease that afflicted Iraqi society by its tyrannical rulers and foreigners who stole the Iraqi identity include the following:

1. That educational institutions and political parties cultivate loyalty to Iraq and not to the ruler who rules.

2. Separation of religion from politics and limiting it to religious institutions only.

3. Politicians are not allowed to use religion in their political activities but rather leave it to the clergy.

4. The application of legal and social justice between nationalities, religions, sects, and tribes without discriminating one over the other.

5. Service towards the citizen and respect for their national and human rights without prejudice and favouring one over the other.

6. Abolishment of the political quotas and replacing them with people of competence, experience, integrity, and transparency.

7. Establishment of political museums in which pictures of the traitorous Iraqi rulers and politicians - their images, corruption, agency and betrayal - are shown in every province in Iraq.

8. Renunciation of dealing with their families in order to be a lesson to others.

9. Confiscation of movable and immovable agents and traitors' money and returning them to the state.

10. Failure to accept the children of traitors and agents in public schools as punishment for their parents' betrayal of the homeland.

11. Refusal to appoint the children of traitors and agents to government jobs as a punishment for what their fathers have done towards the homeland.

References:

1. Al-Omar, Maan Khalil. 1982 "Critique of Contemporary Social Thought" Dar Al Afaq Al Jadeeda - Beirut.

2. Al-Omar, Maan Khalil. 2012 "New Crimes" Dar Wael - Amman.

3. Al-Omar, Maan Khalil. 2016 "Iraq's Ruling Elites" Dar Al-Shorouk - Amman.